To Ian

Happy wa

Stu Bell

Rambling on ...

... and on

Stuart Bell

ISBN 978-1-907257-48-3

Published in 2012 by
Quoin Publishing Ltd.,
17 North Street, Middlesbrough,
England
TS2 1JP

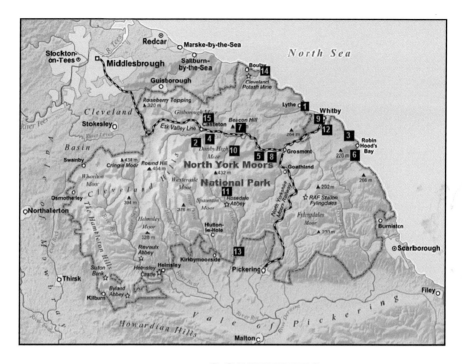

CONTENTS

INTRODUCTION

THE AUTHOR

In the early 1990s I was paid the princely sum of £40 for an article I penned in the football magazine *When Saturday Comes*. It described my longstanding devotion to Berwick Rangers Football Club and the delights of a deep-fried pie – a Scottish delicacy that had oozed over the border and was the snack of choice for anyone minded to ingest 8,000 calories in less than two minutes. (That included several Berwick players and both linesmen). On the strength of that sporting and culinary tome, I was exhorted by some friends to write a book. Twenty years later, here it is!

I was born and grew up in Thornaby and emigrated to Redcar when I married my wife, Julie, in 1986. I went to Westbury Street Junior School and Middlesbrough High School, where my teenage years were shared with female classmates in belt-sized miniskirts that make today's versions look like ball gowns. It is no surprise therefore – indeed it's my only real excuse – that I failed more O-levels than most people sit. This includes two attempts at English language, so if my syntax is dodgy, my infinitives are split and my metaphors get horribly mixed, you know the reason why.

I cobbled together enough certificates to go to Newcastle Polytechnic, where I lasted a full 20 seconds. "Did you not get the letter? Your course is cancelled, mate." I transferred in something of a daze to Sheffield where I didn't last much longer before scuttling back to Thornaby to look for a job.

Ten months at Wimpey's (the builder) as a trainee Quantity Surveyor came and went, because the only quantities they let me loose on were teabags and sugar lumps. However, these important transferrable skills were welcomed at British Rail where I spent 32 largely happy years.

1

As you read the walks in this book, you will note that I often go off on tangents where I rant about some irritant of modern life. Just to illustrate that style, I'm now minded to slip into a tirade about the state of Britain's Railways. You see, when I started with BR in 1975 and for many years afterwards, they operated a reasonably-efficient service at a fraction of the current price, they didn't shut the network down on Bank Holidays, they could add extra services or carriages at very short notice and most stations were manned with heated waiting rooms. They even ran overnight services – virtually unheard of now – though admittedly they were largely for the benefit of shady and inebriated folk living on the margins of society (and that was just the staff).

Now, for ridiculous sums of money, you have the opportunity to wait on vandalised stations, perhaps with a few bits of Perspex for shelter, to board a 30-year-old rust bucket with 500 other people, on which the heaters only work in summer. If it gets stuck at some dodgy points you have to wait three hours for a bloke in an orange jacket to drive down from Carlisle to give them a kick. Then, if you do arrive "on time" (modern railway parlance for ten minutes late), your "connecting" train will cheerfully slam its doors and pull out right in front of you and there won't be another one for two hours. The man with the whistle, without a trace of shame, will say: "Sorry, couldn't hold it, it's a different company," before scuttling off to his office for a coffee and some Hobnobs that he's nicked from the first-class lounge.

Rant over – but you get the drift of my approach to this book.

Anyway, after rail privatisation in the 1990s, there was a reorganisation every Friday afternoon for about ten years. I survived various redundancy threats but eventually took a modest cheque from them when EWS Railway decided in 2006 that it would be a good idea to reduce Thornaby Depot to a pile of rubble. Since then I've done a few part-time jobs, including two years watching what appeared to be a masterclass of corporate self-destruction at Redcar steelworks, but was actually much more complex. Cultural inflexibility, globalisation and other snore-inducing concepts were at play and I was relieved to escape. However, the horrors of daytime TV took over and I was soon glad for an excuse to get out of the house.

THE WHITBY GAZETTE

With all that spare time on my hands, I enjoyed going for walks on the North York Moors, even if it was just an excuse to go to any one of many wonderful pubs in Whitby and the Esk Valley. One day, whilst reading in the *Whitby Gazette* about someone in Sandsend burning his toast, I realised that it didn't have a walking column. Amongst the excellent coverage of local news, gossip, slaggings of Scarborough Council and a rather unhealthy obsession with dog poo, somebody writes about astronomy, there are detailed descriptions of brutal encounters in the local football league and there are adverts for coffee mornings in Ugthorpe.

But, in the midst of some of the most beautiful and spectacular scenery in England, there was no walking column. Most other newspapers have them and to be honest I'm never particularly impressed. They often seem to be written by humourless dullards who conjure up an image that a day out walking is about solitude and chunky sweaters, flasks of tea and waterproof gaiters, the "country code" and muesli bars. Well, if that's your bag, fair

3

enough, but I think it puts many people off, people who would enjoy a bit of fresh air and scenery but also need to know that it's OK to loudly curse your blisters and spend several hours in the pub at the end.

So, I sent the *Gazette* an e.mail telling them that I do the walks anyway and asked would they like me to send a sample article? To my considerable surprise the Editor, Jon Stokoe, said yes and I've been writing the monthly columns now since Autumn 2010.

THE WALKS

As I explained to Jon, I didn't just want to write a descriptive text indicating where people should cross a footbridge or climb over a stile. My inner David Brent wanted to amuse and entertain too, so that it would still be readable for anyone who had no intention of shuffling around Eskdale in the mud for three hours. So yes, the text will describe the route in detail, but it's meant to be amusing too – though only you, the reader, can be a judge of that.

There are 15 walks, all of which have appeared in the *Whitby Gazette*. However, in the newspaper I'm constrained by word count, by the genteel nature of the *Gazette*'s readership, and by the Editor's understandable desire not to upset influential people in the town. In this book though, I've taken those 15 walks and added 400 words or so to each, in order to correct small errors, to increase the waffle factor and to occasionally vent my spleen (whatever that means). I don't think I've added anything particularly insulting or controversial, the intention is just to add extra readability for those couple of hours at the end of the walk in the corner of a cosy pub.

The 15 walks are:

- Mostly circular (three are linear);
- Between five and nine miles long (two to three hours' walking);
- In the North York Moors (coast, country and town);
- Accessible using public transport from Teesside and Whitby;
- On public rights of way (footpaths or quiet country lanes).

Don't blame me if the bus or train service I used is withdrawn by the time you read this. The bus may be gone, but the walk is still there. So you'll have to use your car.

I try to use some of the less well known paths wherever possible and this may mean additional mud, missing waymarks and camouflaged stiles, but they are not difficult. Also, apart from one or two serious climbs up the sides of valleys, this is not the Himalayas. You may occasionally gasp for air whilst admiring a view, but if this clapped-out collection of arthritic joints can make it, so can you.

THE MAPS

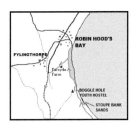

I cobble my own maps together using *Microsoft Paint*. They are not particularly to scale and since I had no intention of writing a book when I first started drawing them, they are not exactly consistent. Some of the shadings and fonts differ from map to map. But hey, they take ages and I'm not doing them all again. So there. They aren't exactly Ordnance Survey standard, but if you use them in conjunction with the text, you shouldn't go wrong.

The best maps in the world are the two-and-a-half-inch OS leisure maps, and I would advise that you take the right one with you, just in case. All of the walks in this book are on the Ordnance Survey Explorer maps OL26 (Western) or OL27 (Eastern) double-sided maps of the North York Moors.

PHOTOGRAPHS

They're all my own work and a quick flick through the book will show you the sort of terrain you're dealing with. There are hills and becks and farmyards and, as in the title of the Daniel Day-Lewis film, there will be mud. They've been inserted in the text at the moment you should be able to see the same view, but the sheep may have moved somewhere else …

The pictures also betray the time of year I did the walks. The scene below – in Fryupdale – was clearly taken in winter. But that's the thing about the North York Moors, you can do these walks in each of the four seasons and have a very different experience each time. The scenery and the colours change dramatically, and I always find it difficult to say which season is best. A crisp winter's day with snow blanketing the tops? Warm summer sunshine and tractors making hay? Purple heather and russet trees in autumn? Green shoots and birdsong in spring? It's all wonderful, really. 60 walks for the price of 15!

Winter in Fryupdale.

And finally ...

CLOTHING AND WEATHER

Check the weather forecast and wear appropriate clothing. Er, that's about it really! Waterproof boots aren't as expensive as they used to be and are highly recommended in anything other than a Saharan drought. Apart from the boots, Murphy's Law applies to British weather and you will either carry six pullovers around with you all day or will end up looking enviously at the sheep. If it rains, you will get wet. If it snows you will feel cold. If the wind blows, your new hair-do will be ruined (though mine is usually OK).

THAT PESKY COUNTRY CODE

Leave everything as you find it and take your litter home. You are allowed to make offensive gestures towards the nearest farmhouse if you find barbed wire over a stile.

SAFETY

Inspired by the "Caution – wet floor" sign in my local swimming pool, here are my three top safety tips.

- Don't strip naked before rolling around in nettles.
- When confronted by a *Ribena*-faced farmer with a shotgun and a snarling dog, don't ask him if he wants to join the Hunt Saboteurs Association.
- Refrain from saying: "Come on then, if you think you're hard enough," to a snorting bull.

I'm a qualified Health and Safety Manager, and you'll ignore these three important pieces of advice at your own peril. Now, get your boots on, pick a walk, and get out there. May I wish you good weather, nature at its best, and happy feet.

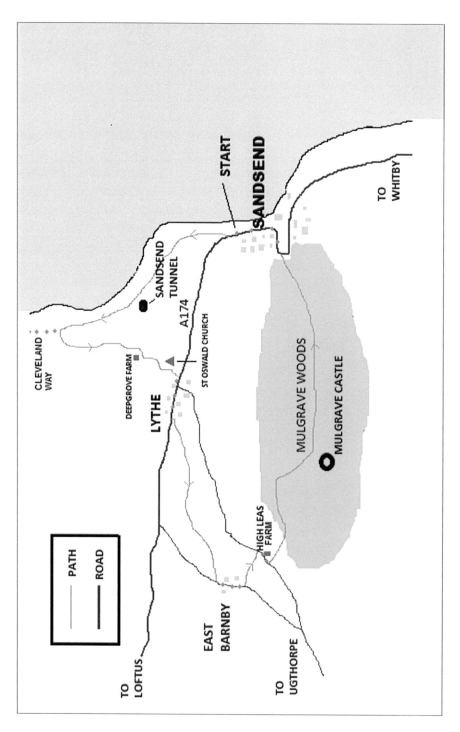

Sandsend

DISTANCE: 8 MILES
APPROX. TIME: 3 HOURS
STARTING POINT: CAR PARK, BOTTOM OF LYTHE BANK

This is a circular walk of about eight miles, offering sea cliffs, mature woodland and supermodel Elle McPherson. It starts from the car park behind the excellent Wit's End cafe at Sandsend, where Arriva's No.5 bus from Middlesbrough will drop you after a hair-raising descent of Lythe bank. By all means take time to calm down and fuel up with a cappuccino and a toasted teacake.

One hundred yards into the car park, climb the

Sandsend Ness.

steps on your left up to the trackbed of the disused Whitby to Saltburn railway and head right, away from the village. Soon you will pass a footpath on your left which climbs up more steeply than the stairway to heaven and, if you are prone to nosebleeds, you are advised to ignore it now and for the rest of your life. Carry on along the old trackbed for a mile or so until you reach the bricked-up entrance to Sandsend Tunnel. This is just one of a series of major engineering feats that were required to build the line, but which ultimately contributed to its early demise. The line was so structurally challenged by landslips, flimsy viaducts and dodgy tunnels that it didn't even survive long enough for the dreaded Dr. Beeching to snip it triumphantly from the UK railway map in the 1960s. (The last train ran on 5th May, 1958).

Those of you who paid attention when reading this book's introduction, will recall that I worked for the railway for 32 years and my first boss at Thornaby repair shed told me a story to illustrate how Sandsend Tunnel saved Beeching from an

Sandsend Tunnel.

extra few minutes' work. If you could walk through it, you'd realise that the roof leaks like a two-bob tent, and it was no better half a century ago. My boss described a journey one winter's morning where the lines were so wet and slippery in the mile-long tunnel that the engine couldn't cope with the rising gradient. Two attempts resulted in the train wheezing to a halt half-way through, so he backed up almost to Whitby, shouted: "Geronimo," and took a run at it. Nearly at the top of the gradient, the drive wheels began spinning wildly on the greasy rails and with the tunnel and cab now thick with black smoke he finally conceded defeat. After sliding back to Sandsend, the Station Master took one look at the semi-asphyxiated crew and called an ambulance.

Table 26 SCARBOROUGH, WHITBY, GUISBOROUGH, BATTERSBY and MIDDLESBROUGH

Week Days only

Miles	Bradshaw - October 1950	a.m	a.m	a.m		a.m	a.m.	a.m	a.m	a.m		p.m S		noon	p.m	p.m.		p.m	p.m	p.m	p.m	p.m
	24Hull .... dep	..	..	..	..	..	..	5 30	..	..	..	..	..	..	8 35	..	..	..	2 25	..	..	5 45
	29York .... "	..	..	..	..	..	..	4 30	..	..	..	..	..	..	1015	..	..	..	2 55	..	..	6 25
—	Scarborough (Cen.) dep	..	..	..	..	TC 16 Middlesbrough	..	8 12	TC to Middlesbrough	..	..	..	..	..	1140	..	..	..	4 35	..	..	8 15
2¾	Scalby	..	..	..	..		..	8 27		..	..	..	..	..	1154	..	..	..	4 49	..	..	..
5	Cloughton	..	..	..	..		..	8 32		..	..	..	..	..	12 3	..	..	..	4 54	..	..	8 34
7	Hayburn Wyke	..	..	..	..		..	8 37		..	..	..	..	..	12 8	..	..	..	4 59	..	..	8 39
8	Stainton Dale	..	..	..	..		..	8 41		..	..	..	..	..	1217	..	..	..	5 3	..	..	8 43
10½	Ravenscar	..	..	..	..		..	8 51		..	..	..	..	..	1221	..	..	..	5 12	..	..	8 52
13½	Fyling Hall	..	..	..	..		..	8 59		..	..	..	..	..	1229	..	..	..	5 20	..	..	9 0
15½	Robin Hood's Bay	..	..	..	..		..	9 4		..	..	..	..	..	1234	..	..	..	5 25	..	..	9 5
18½	Hawsker	..	..	..	..		..	9 13		..	..	..	..	..	1243	..	..	..	5 34	..	..	9 14
21½	Whitby West Cliff .. arr	..	..	..	..		..	9 20		..	..	..	..	..	1250	..	..	..	5 41	..	..	9 21
23½	28Whitby .... arr	..	..	..	..		..	9 33	..	..	..	..	..	..	..	..	..	..	..	..	..	9 32
	dep	..	..	6 45	..	6 52	..	..	9 10	..	..	..	..	12 0	..	..	..	4 0	..	..	5 50	..
—	Whitby West Cliff . dep	..	..	..	..	7 0	..	TC Scarborough to Whitby	9 21	..	..	..	..	TC to Middlesbrough	1232	..	..	TC to Middlesbrough	5 45	..	..	..
24	Sandsend	..	..	..	..	7 6	..		9 30	..	..	..	..		1238	..	..		5 51	..	..	..
26½	Kettleness	..	..	..	..	7 14	..		9 35	..	..	..	..		1 6	..	..		5 58	..	..	..
30	Hinderwell for Runswick	..	..	..	..	7 22	..		9 46	..	..	..	..		1 14	..	..		6 7	..	..	..
31½	Staithes .... [Bay	..	..	..	..	7 28	..		9 51	..	..	..	..		1 19	..	..		6 17	..	..	..
36½	Loftus	..	..	..	..	7 46	..		10 8	..	..	..	..		1 35	..	..		6 32	..	..	..
37½	Skinningrove	..	..	..	..	7 50	..		1012	..	..	..	..		1 39	..	..		6 36	..	..	..
41½	Brotton	..	..	..	..	8 1	..		1023	10 35	..	..	..		1 50	..	..		6 47	6 55	..	..
44	North Skelton	..	..	..	..	..	..		..	10 40	..	..	..		..	..	..		..	7 1	..	..
46½	54Saltburn .... arr	..	..	..	..	..	..		..	10 52	..	..	..		..	..	..		..	7 18	..	..
44	Boosbeck	..	..	..	..	8 9	..	..	1031	..	..	..	..	..	1 58	..	..	..	6 53	..	..	..
48	Guisborough .... arr	..	..	..	..	8 18	..		1040	..	..	..	..	..	2 8	..	..	..	7 4	..	..	..
	dep	5 0	7 20	..	..	8 19	9 10	..	1041	..	..	1248	..	..	2 9	4 12	..	..	7 5	..	..	..
49½	Hutton Gate	5 4	7 24	..	..	8 23	9 14	..	1045	..	..	1252	..	..	2 13	4 16	..	..	7 9	..	..	..
50½	Pinchinthorpe	..	7 28	..	..	8 27	9 18	..	1049	..	..	1256	..	..	2 17	4 20	..	..	7 13	..	..	..
—	Battersby	..	..	8 10	..	..	..	..	..	..	..	..	..	1 24	..	..	..	5 20	..	..	7 20	..
—	2¾ Great Ayton	..	..	8 17	..	..	..	..	..	..	..	..	..	1 31	..	..	..	5 27	..	..	7 27	..
53½	Nunthorpe	5 12	7 34	8 25	..	8 33	9 24	..	1055	..	..	1 2	..	1 39	2 23	4 26	..	5 35	7 19	..	7 35	..
55	Ormesby	5 16	7 38	8 29	..	8 37	9 28	..	1059	..	..	1 6	..	1 43	2 27	4 30	..	5 39	7 23	..	7 39	..
58	Middlesbrough ..... arr	5 22	7 44	8 36	..	8 43	9 34	..	1112	..	..	1 12	..	1 49	2 33	4 36	..	5 46	7 29	..	7 45	..
73	34Darlington ..... arr	6 10	8 22	9 22	..	9 22	10 40	..	1214	..	..	2 37	..	2 37	3 16	5 48	..	6 48	8 8	..	8 43	..
105½	65Newcastle 2 .... "	7 42	9 31	..	..	1051	..	..	1257	..	..	2 56	..	3 56	4 53	6 53	..	8 51	9 41	..	9 41	..

The easy(ish) route for you is up a long flight of stairs to the right of the tunnel. At the top, making a similar noise to that steam engine, go straight on along a wide track. After half-a-mile, the cliffs pop over to see you from the right, but you should turn sharp left at a signpost

Kettle Ness.

for Lythe, though not before pausing to look at the stunning view towards Kettleness. At the end of this field, cross a stile into a narrow tract of woodland, then go over a footbridge before climbing back out of the woods to head up to Deepgrove Farm. Keep all the farm buildings on your right then

Mulgrave Estate Woodland

OPEN TO ACCESS ON FOOT ON

Saturday,Sunday and Wednesday only

Closed throughout MAY

DOGS STRICTLY ON LEADS

Please take all your litter home

follow the wide track at the rear which eventually emerges onto the road at the top of Lythe Bank near the pretty St. Oswald's church.

They mean "Welcome to Mulgrave Woods – have a great day."

Now, if any of the following criteria are true, you can turn left and head down the bank back to Sandsend:

- It's May, or it's Monday, Tuesday, Thursday or Friday in any other month (the only days you're allowed onto our planned path through Mulgrave Woods);
- You've already examined the rest of this chapter and prefer to get home while it's still light;
- There's a large black cloud on the horizon, and you didn't want to come out in the first place. Do please carry on by heading right until you

Entrance to Mulgrave Woods.

reach the Football Federation premises at the end of Lythe village on the other side of the road. Take the signposted path that runs parallel to the road and follow it as it skirts around a fabulously pristine football pitch. Having raced athletically down the right wing, turn right through three successive gates and follow a clear path for a mile until you emerge from the trees over a stile into a field. Head straight over to the buildings opposite and turn left down the road in the village of East Barnby. Half-a-mile later, at a wooden seat (where you may choose to stop to admire the view), turn onto a path which hugs a fence on the left, then heads into an area of thin woodland before dropping down to High Leas Farm. Turn right on the road, but quickly left again down a signposted path that is as wet as a nightclub carpet. (Anyone remember the "Claggy Mat" in 1970s Middlesbrough?)

At the bottom of the slope, head through a gate on the left marked "Mulgrave Estate". This won't be the only time you see such a sign in these parts. The Mulgrave Estate amounts to 15,000 acres of land stretching four miles along the coast and nine miles inland, on which a variety of wild animals can be blasted into oblivion by fat businessmen convinced that they are indulging in sport. The paradox of a townie wanting to live in the countryside is that you'd have to share it with so many people who are happiest when peppering some frightened bird with shotgun pellets. Wildlife is one of the biggest attractions for me, and I just don't get the notion that it's a great day out to destroy some of it. And to call it hunting – please, spare me. Standing in a line, sipping from a silver hip flask, whilst someone drives the birds in the general direction of a dozen guns, well, it's hardly a safari is it?

This grand pile is the seat of one Constantine

Edmund Walter Phipps, 5th Marquess of Normanby, who is reputedly worth the not inconsiderable sum of £143m. So, you may think he could afford to spend a few quid on waymarks to help you navigate your way through Mulgrave Woods. There are numerous paths, but many are for the use of the Estate's gamekeepers and go around in circles, or lead up to a locked gate at the perimeter of the wood. Enter the woods and head left on the track leading up to a fence on the edge of the wood. (The OS map suggests you head right, but I've tried that several times and gone horribly wrong each time). You eventually need to head down to the valley floor, so when you see a track going right, take it and head downhill, but don't double back on yourself. You may get the distinct impression that the Estate Managers prefer you to enter from the Sandsend entrance. It's a bit The-Prisoner-meets-Hotel-California and maybe there are a bunch of blokes in white coats watching you on giant screens up at the Castle, ready to release the dogs should you make a bid for freedom.

Tunnel in Mulgrave woods.

Now, having said all that, I'm really not trying to put you off. Indeed, I implore you to persevere, as you will be rewarded with a lovely walk through mature deciduous woodland – beautiful in any season but particularly so in autumn and pretty as a picture in springtime too. Also, it's fair to say that the only times I've had an encounter with any of the Estate's staff, they've been exceptionally helpful and polite. (And it was a Thursday … !)

Old Mulgrave Castle.

Elle McPherson? Well, "The Body" and lingerie specialist apparently leased the estate and castle for four months a few years back and who knows whether she enjoyed herself enough to repeat the exercise. Perhaps she soon scuttled back to her pad in London when, out for a stroll in the woods,

she was spooked by an old bald geezer from Redcar lurking in the bushes and staring glumly at his map.

After about 15 minutes, your route should bring you out onto a wide track which turns further downhill and right over a weir.

The track heads through a long tunnel and then heads left again, but I recommend that you go back just a short way and go up the hill to explore the ruins of the 13th century Mulgrave Castle (Elle McPherson got the new one near Lythe). Back on the track, always keep the stream on your right, and you will emerge, punching the air, at a woodyard in Sandsend.

Your reward is a cream tea in Woodside Eats cafe on your left or a pint in the Hart pub away to your right. To complete the circle, head left along the road (beware crashing waves at high tide!) back to the car park/ bus stop at Wit's End Cafe.

Sandsend exit from Mulgrave Woods

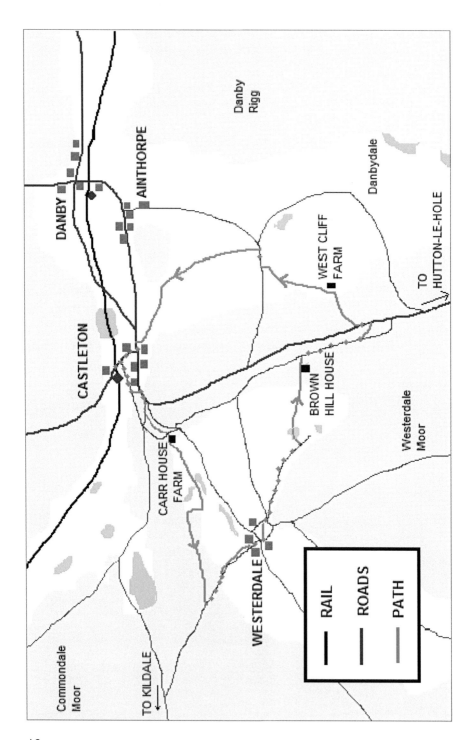

Westerdale

DISTANCE: 8 MILES
APPROX. TIME: 3 HOURS
STARTING POINT: CASTLETON STATION

The Esk Valley walk, as you may shrewdly guess, follows the River Esk from its boggy source to its last fun-filled 200 yards past the amusements in Whitby. The Eskdale way is a much longer circumnavigation of the moors on either side of the river. Commendable as they are, both miss large swathes of the broad and beautiful valleys to the South of the Esk which, collectively and alliteratively, I'll call the Eskdale Extensions. There are four of them and all feature in separate walks in this book.

Westerdale is the furthest of the four from Whitby, at the head of the catchment area for the River Esk. This walk is a circular route from Castleton, so you can drive or use the Esk Valley train service. It is approximately eight miles, though can be curtailed to about five by inventing some flimsy excuse and escaping down the road from Westerdale village.

Walk uphill through the main road in Castleton and as it bears left on its litter- and mutton-strewn route towards Hutton-le-Hole, a minor road goes straight on to Westerdale. Immediately take a path to the right running parallel to the road. This pleasant grassy track runs eastwards for a mile and enjoys increasingly lovely views of Eskdale dropping away to the right and Westerdale muscling in from the left. As you meet a wall on the left, follow it down to the road, then straight over and down a path adjacent to Carr House. Clearly a fan of Steptoe and Son (ask your dad), the landowner has assembled a vast collection of breeze blocks and scrap wood for you to admire as you head on to cross a concrete bridge, then left on a rising incline to a gate.

The recently-diverted path takes you through a new plantation of native trees (beware of some landslips and invasive broom bushes), then out through a gate onto a wide track.

Turn uphill and follow the waymark sharp right at a gate, then through a second gate in the opposite corner of the field. Walk diagonally uphill for 100 yards to a final gate, then left alongside a wall. It's

The mark I gained in my last English exam … with Westerdale in the distance.

left again as you follow the wall and a stand of pine trees, but as civilisation drops away to your left the path bears right into the heather and, after a mile or so, spits you out onto a minor road.

This straight road drops down to Westerdale Village, which emerges in a dramatic fashion over the brow of a hill. Shortly after a cattle grid, and a track on the left towards Fir Trees House, take a grass path on the left running parallel to the road. This route rewards you by crossing the stream over

Hunter's Sty bridge.

the hidden gem of Hunters Sty packhorse bridge, somewhat preferable to the ford on the road.

Go uphill into the almost spookily quiet village. Eskvalley.com list the amenities here as "a church, a toilet and a public phone", but there's just a chance life may be transformed in the coming years. As I write, an oil and gas exploration company has applied for permission for an exploratory borehole near Westerdale, presumably because the geology suggests it's sitting on something large and flammable. Strange that they make such finds in tranquil retreats like this rather than under some run-down estate in Doncaster.

Now is the time to feel a twinge in your hamstring if you wish to avoid the steep climb ahead and escape back to Castleton down the next turning on the left. Otherwise, it's straight on past the strikingly attractive Christ's Church, then left down Lead Lane. After ten yards go through a gate on your right then

Christ's Church, Westerdale.

diagonally left to a stone stile, then on to a second stone stile in the far corner of the next field which would hopelessly fail a Health and Safety audit.

And Lord help us if the H&S police that wander around our towns, cities and workplaces are ever let loose on the footpaths of Britain. They'd shut most of them down and half of the country would be decorated with red and white ribbon as they zealously tape off perceived hazards. The entire pier at Berwick-upon-Tweed has been closed for months by men in yellow jackets and bump hats, and yet some precipitous goat track can remain open to all-comers. A few years ago I was gullible enough to walk up to Sharp Edge in the Lake District in a howling gale and driving rain. I didn't start to question the sanity of a friend who led this little expedition, until I was clinging to a narrow ridge with a 500-foot drop on either side. Twenty yards ahead of me, I was expected to stand on a sloping wedge of rock with as much grip as a bar of Palmolive, then leap across a gully to the next available handhold. So convinced was I that I was about to die, I reached into my rucksack, took out my sandwiches and gulped them down because it would be a shame to let them go to waste. Fortunately, another friend walking just behind me, caved in and after emitting some alarming gurgling noises declared that he was not going an inch further. His actions made me look slightly less like a sissy as we all scuttled back down the way we came, though on the other hand I had nothing left to eat when we stopped for lunch down in the valley.

Anyhow, the point is that nobody stopped me doing that – it's a public footpath – but shove a cardboard box under the stairs in the office whilst you go back to lock the car boot, and a small army of men with clipboards will be waiting for you when

you get back, tutting away and gibbering on about   View to Castleton Rigg.
fire extinguishers. My last two years on the railway
were as a Health and Safety Manager and let me tell
you that 99 per cent of the law is correct, but the
average H&S Manager is a self-obsessed twonk who
spends most of his time on trivia, whilst ignoring the
serious stuff because most of the budget has gone
on his salary.

Phew. OK, that stile is a bit iffy but you'll get round it one way or another to turn right along the road for half-a-mile, then left on a path shortly before the farm building. Before reaching the trees, go right through a gate then over a footbridge, shortly after which I was almost mown down by two deer leaping out of the woods, which then had the temerity to stop and giggle at me as I tried to retrieve my hat from a hawthorn bush.

Head steadily uphill now for some distance, bearing slightly right through a series of fields to reach Brown Hill House. Zig-zag up the hill beyond the farm until you reach the road leading up towards Castleton Rigg. Take a last look back at gorgeous Westerdale (and it truly is a wonderful view), then follow the road uphill. Keep your eyes open for the main Castleton road away on your left, and as soon as you see it, cut across the heather to join it and head left admiring the dazzling beauty of the next Eskdale extension – Danby Dale. Soon, a footpath sign indicates a steep descent down a slippery-when-wet gully to West Cliff Farm.

We'll visit Danby Dale again in another chapter, so for today, we'll take the easy but still quiet and appealing route back to Castleton. At West Cliff Farm, turn left on its access track down the valley, which soon turns into a tiny road at Plum Tree Farm. After half-a-mile, turn right at a junction and up a steep hill then, with a church away to your right, take a minor road left. This is a gated road called Wandels Lane and will take you straight back into the centre of Castleton Village where the pubs, shops and cafes await the safe return of your wallet.

View back down Wandel's Lane to Danbydale.

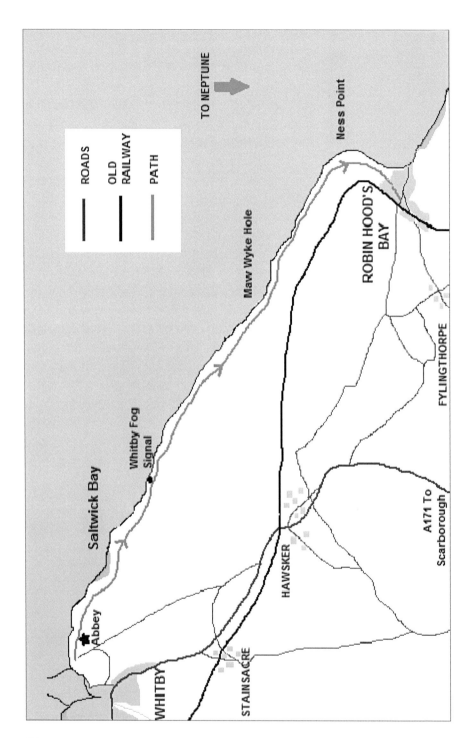

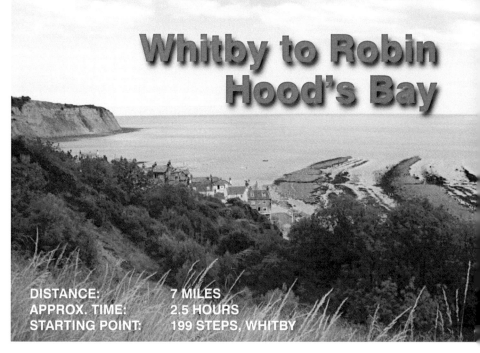

Whitby to Robin Hood's Bay

DISTANCE: 7 MILES
APPROX. TIME: 2.5 HOURS
STARTING POINT: 199 STEPS, WHITBY

It would not be unusual to find me somewhere on the moors, staring angrily at a map, convinced that it had accidentally stopped under the wrong nozzle at the printers. For instance, I blamed the map when I followed a line of flattened grass down a long hill confident it was my footpath, only to find that it had been created by an oil drum in the bushes at the bottom.

It's rewarding when you get the map reading right, but sometimes you just want to switch off, enjoy the scenery and the fresh air, and let the well-trodden path beneath your feet lead you to your destination.

The day before this walk, I had to take our lovely old cat Jessie to be put to sleep. She was delivered to us 20 years earlier by two small boys who knocked on the door and said "Is this your kitten?" "I suppose she is now," I replied, as they handed over a bundle of fur, wheezing away and barely alive. She survived that and a couple of other bouts of flu, two poisonings, ripped ligaments, various other

Jess.

serious ailments and for the last seven years, diabetes.

My wife and I have had pet cats all our lives, but Jess was a special character. She was clever, pretty, inquisitive and loving, had a greater vocabulary than some humans I know and purred like a Harley-Davidson. If she wanted anything, like a catnip toy that was hidden at the back of the cupboard, a piece of your dinner, or the middle of the settee, then she persevered till she got it. 20 years is a good age for a cat, but that doesn't make losing her any easier. Frankly, there just aren't enough hankies in the world.

This is an easy, seven-mile lost-in-your-thoughts stroll down the Cleveland Way to Robin Hood's Bay. Head up the 199 steps below the Abbey, and straight on past the church, then bear left at the Abbey entrance and left again at a Cleveland Way sign saying "Robin Hoods Bay 6.5 miles". Skirt left past a wooden gate displaying the welcoming instruction in

It says: "Trespassers will be shot".
Best keep to the left!

red paint "Keep out – trespassers will be shot".

As you marvel at the diversity of human nature, take a look over your shoulder at the lovely view back to Sandsend, then carry on along the cliff top.

Saltwick Bay.

After a mile, pass through the centre of Saltwick Bay Caravan Park and as the tarmac curls away right, go straight on back to the cliff top path. 20 minutes later you'll approach the enormous old fog horns which would surely have your fillings out if someone set them off as you passed by.

The path then turns right up to the bracken as it passes the old lighthouse (now a holiday home), then resumes its journey along the cliffs.

Old lighthouse and fog station.

It was on a muddy stretch around this point that I slid off the path onto the hard shoulder and literally stumbled over an empty can. It was an *HP* "All Day Breakfast", consisting of (and I use the following terms loosely) some bacon, two sausages, three button mushrooms and two pork and egg nuggets all swimming around in a puddle of baked beans.

Now, some people take a packed lunch or maybe a Mars Bar to snack on along the way, so you could spend some time musing over the mentality of someone whose energy boost comes from a chemistry set masquerading as a breakfast. You may also muse, as I did, that the chances of stumbling over a bloke with tomato sauce in his beard, clutching his stomach and groaning pitifully, had now significantly increased. What really perplexed me though was the notion that having eaten it, the gastronomic connoisseur then thought it would be a good idea to chuck the empty tin into the long grass. I'd previously conducted an in-depth investigation into wayside litter and because this easy walk needs little description and I have space to fill, I include it at the end of this chapter.

Carrying on, there are a few dips and climbs to negotiate – but nothing too strenuous – as you continue admiring the sea birds, the stunning cliff scenery and (allegedly) migrating whales out at sea. A number of paths head inland (including one marked by a luminous yellow arrow imploring you to head for the railway route), but you should always stick to the path heading along the cliff edge.

Finally, as you head around Bay Ness, a magnificent view of Robin Hood's Bay emerges, with Ravenscar's huge cliffs further South. The path brings you out on to Mount Pleasant North Road, at the end of which turn left to head past the shop (the 93 bus back to Whitby comes down Thorpe Lane

View from the path to Robin Hood's Bay.

opposite) and then down the hill to the pubs, cafes and gift shops of this picturesque old village.

For me, knees aching, I didn't get further than the real ale of the Victoria Hotel, which must have one of the world's best beer garden views. However, I did this walk in February so an outside seat wasn't really an option and I chose instead to camp in front of the coal fire in the bar.

I suspect, Jessie would have agreed with that.

Litter – the final score

Last summer, whilst walking along a short stretch of the road along Castleton Rigg, I was so shocked at the amount of litter that I found myself cataloguing it in a mildly obsessive manner. Using advanced number-crunching techniques, (biro, beer mat), I figured that from this sample I could calculate the total volume of litter ejected through car windows across the whole of the North York Moors.

The methodology I used was to multiply the figure up by the total length of road on the OS Eastern map, (so if for example I'd checked the litter on 1 mile of road and there are 126 miles of road I'd multiply my findings by 126). I realised I needed to take the amount of traffic on each road into account so I weighted A roads at x1.5, B roads at x1 and C roads at x0.5. Then I multiplied it by two because my sample was only on one side of the road, then multiplied it again by four as there are four sides to the OS maps of the North York Moors. These last two calculations mean that all these resulting figures are divisible by eight and I mention this just in case some pedant spots it and thinks it looks suspicious. (This means you, Jez Summers!).

Without further ado, here are the NYM litter awards for 2010:

	TOTAL
Soft drinks (plastic bottles)	33,656
Lager cans	13,864
Fag packets	11,888
Miscellaneous plastic containers	11,880
Crisp packets	9,904
Sweet wrappers	7,920
Beer bottles	7,912
Soft drinks (cans)	5,936
Carrier bags	3,976
Milk cartons	3,960
Soiled nappies (no, honest)	2,208
Fag ends	several million

And this is just a small margin near the roadside – carrier bags, sweet wrappers, and the like, will blow away some distance into the heather.

For the interests and bonus claims of any local sales reps, the winners in some of the fields include *Stella Artois* (bottled beer category), *Carling Black Label* (cans), *Walkers Cheese and Onion Crisps* and *Lambert and Butler* ciggies. Special mention though to *Lucozade* which was well up there in the plastic bottles category, yet was only used medicinally when I was a lad. Congratulations to you all.

So don't forget folks, when out for a drive in the country – presumably because you like the scenery – and you fancy a sugary drink and some plastic sausages, throw most of it out on the A roads or it will devalue my comprehensive research.

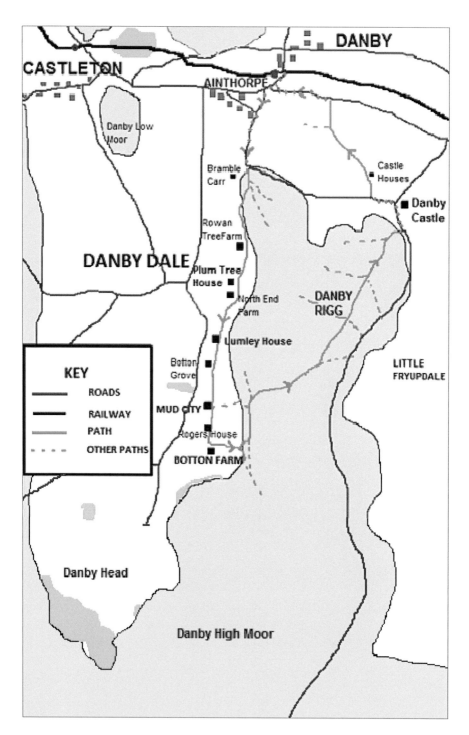

Danby Dale

DISTANCE: 7.5 MILES
APPROX. TIME: 3 HOURS
STARTING POINT: DANBY STATION

I did this walk on the warmest day of early spring and it was refreshing to see the emergence of some bright green tinges and later, up on Danby Rigg, to hear several skylarks twittering away as they haggled over the best nesting sites.

Start at Danby station turning right along the main road, then up the hill into the village of Ainthorpe. Take the second minor road left, (signposted for the Fox and Hounds and Fryup) and stay on the road uphill past the pub until reaching the tennis courts.

As the road bears left, take a grass path ahead

Don't mess with geese – especially the one in the middle.

on the far right – five yards to the right of a clearer path in a gully. Resist any other paths edging left and go through a gate that is in worse nick than my left knee. Head straight along a path that is fairly distinct and where it vanishes in a few boggy areas just plod on at the same level until it reappears. Once or twice it veers down to inspect a wall or to get a closer look at a farm, but quickly turns away to resume its journey south. If you come to a wall with no clear way through, don't head off to a distant gate – just take a closer look and you will invariably see a stone stile almost hidden in the structure right in front of you. You'll need to clamber over half-a-dozen of these structures along the valley side and whilst they're not as easy to spot as their wooden counterparts, there is usually some faint yellow blob on the stones to show you that you are on the right track.

Stone stile.

The track is obvious until you approach the entrance of North End Farm, then it veers left on a wide track, through a gate, past two old gateposts and right past the remains of an old wall ahead of you. Then pick your way through a jumble of rocks amidst a bubbling spring and head diagonally right to find a stone stile hidden around the corner of the wall on the far side of the field. Leap like a gazelle over a small stream before going right towards Lumley House.

Twenty yards up from the farm building, a waymarked gate leads into a field guarded by two large bovine bouncers of indeterminate gender, wearing Viking headgear and staring in a menacing fashion. Well, trust me, it's all front. They just ignored me as I strode gingerly past and didn't stir even when I sped impressively off into the distance.

The author demonstrating how an elephant might negotiate a stone stile.

A mile further on you reach East Cliff Farm where four horses plodding around in a pond of mud and slurry looked as appalled as I was with underfoot conditions. However, adjacent to the farm buildings

Bovine bouncers.

where you are directed by waymarks to trudge through the deep end, avoid foot rot by staying in the grassy field to the left of the wall and rejoin the path through a gate before going immediately left over a stile into the next field.

Carry on ahead to the left of the bakery of Botton Farm. Botton Village – it's worthy of the village name as it houses 230 people and spreads some distance further up the dale – is a community run by the Camphill Village Trust, a charity which supports adults with learning disabilities, mental health problems and other special needs. There are actually five farms and a number of cottages, though it's essentially a working community producing cheese, jams, biscuits, candles and wooden and glassware.

The Camphill movement was founded by Austrian paediatrician Karl Konig, who fled to Scotland from Vienna in 1938 when Hitler set off on his round-the-world trip. The alpine connections still exist and I got a reminder of this when descending from Danby Rigg to the farm on a hot day about 15 years ago. Leaning on a fence at the bottom of the path, was an old gentleman dressed in lederhosen, woolly socks, a green felt hat with a feather in it and smoking a big curly ceramic pipe. I thought the heat had maybe got to me, but I soon realised that whilst he looked rather unusual, his appearance was considerably more attractive than the sweat streaked apparition that had staggered out of the bracken in front of him accompanied by a large cloud of flies.

At the next wide track, go left up the hill, through a gate, then diagonally right up to another gate. You can follow the signposted-path continuing to the right but you can also save half-a-mile by heading left at the signpost instead and quickly taking a path which curls away to the top of the hill through a shallow gully.

Either way, as your path suddenly flattens out at the top, take a thin track sharp left along the ridge. The stunning views across and down Danbydale more than justify the exertion of the climb.

Upper Danbydale.

After ten minutes or so, as you meet a trail rising up from East Cliff Farm down in the valley, go straight on but after another 30 yards take the path that strikes out right across the moors towards two stone cairns in the distance.

As quickly as the view of Danbydale recedes behind you, so an equally stunning vista emerges

Across to Great Fryupdale.

ahead. Great Fryupdale is away in the distance and is so called because an ancient bylaw dictates that if you knock on any door in the dale before 9.00am, the occupants are legally obliged to cook you a full English. (Er, don't quote me).

As your path begins to drop steeply down, take another, running to your left across the edge of Danby Rigg. Stay on it for two miles or so – resisting two wide cross paths – until you come to a wall almost at the end of the rigg. Turn sharp right down towards the road in Little Fryupdale, (so called because you only get one egg).

Turn left along the road and you soon come to

Little Fryupdale.

Danby Castle, once the home of the feisty Catherine Parr (pictured right). She was named after Catherine of Aragon because her mother, Maud, was a lady in waiting to Henry the Eighth's first wife. Later she became the King's sixth wife (I suspect she didn't do a risk assessment), broke some sort of record by outliving him, and went on to marry the brother of Jane Seymour, Henry's third wife. In fact, perhaps it's the King who should have done a bit of due diligence, because Catherine had already been married twice before she leapt into Henry's bed and both of her previous husbands had died after less than 10 years together. Perhaps Eastenders isn't so far-fetched after all. Fittingly though, after all that wedding cake, the ruined castle is now a marriage venue in a spectacular and beautiful setting.

Follow the road round, and 50 yards past the road junction, head down a field path towards a newly-extended barn, then left to a gate, up through the middle of the next field to a signpost next to the hedge, left to a stile and right down a short tarmacked stretch to the road. Turn left here to go back along the road to Ainthorpe, and then right to return to Danby.

The village of Westerdale (chapter 2 – what do you mean, you skipped it?) makes Danby look like Las Vegas, but it is nevertheless a quiet and pretty little place. It boasts a fine bakery, a health food shop and one of my favourite pubs in the world, the

Danby Castle.

Duke of Wellington. Recently, I was sat chatting to Charlie the barman, when we were interrupted by a low rumbling noise which quickly turned into a loud 'Whoosh!' as an old (and empty) bird's nest fell down the chimney. It was so tinder dry that when it hit the hot coals it positively exploded in flames and a huge cloud of smoke and soot erupted from the fireplace, spreading through the bar in seconds. I just managed to swig my bitter off before it turned into stout, but I had to go home for a bath leaving Charlie vainly trying to clear up the mess with a dustpan and brush. I mention this because it would display great wit and a mature sense of humour, if you were to pop in and rub your finger over the windowsill before shaking your head in disgust. In fact, I bet Charlie would think it's so funny, he'd buy you a free pint.

Danbydale. What a place eh? I've blagged you a full English breakfast and a free pint! This book's already paid for itself!

Duke of Wellington, Danby.

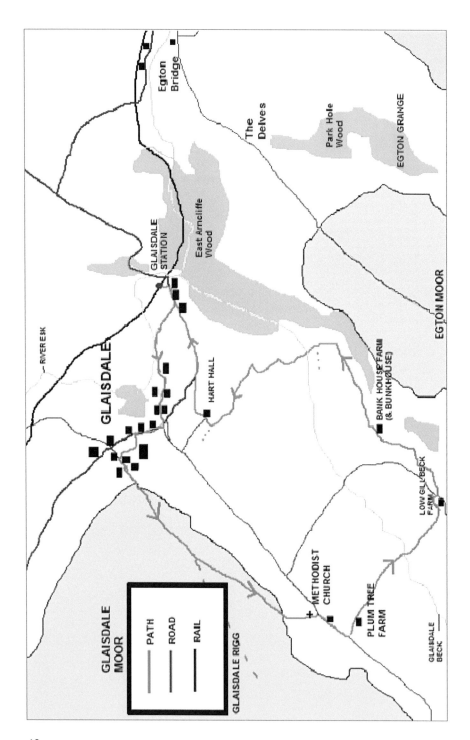

Glaisdale

DISTANCE: 6 MILES
APPROX. TIME: 2.5 HOURS
STARTING POINT: GLAISDALE STATION

This is a six-mile circular walk around Glaisdale – the most easterly of the beautiful and tranquil extensions of Eskdale. I started from Glaisdale station on a fabulously warm March day and was positively assaulted by springtime throughout a walk which was a joy from start to finish.

Head up the hill and turn right onto the back road at the Arncliffe Arms, nodding agreeably at the "open all day, every day" sign. A rookery high in the treetops assailed me with noise as the occupants repaired the eaves and dusted the windowsills in last year's nests, and a local cat smirked knowingly at me as I began the surprisingly steep climb up to the village centre.

Turn right on the main road, and go through a gate in the wall opposite the butcher's shop, then head right and uphill before turning left after the cattle grid. You won't find one of them in the middle of a housing estate in Teesside (and if you did,

*Traffic jam on
Glaisdale Rigg.*

someone would nick it and sell it to a dodgy scrap
dealer along with several hundred yards of signalling
cable and some manhole covers). The gradient soon
eases as the tarmac fizzles out into a rough track
before passing through a gate onto open moorland
and curving left past a large pond.

*At this point I was stopped in my tracks by a
cacophony of quacking, and I searched in vain for
broods of mallards in the reeds. Nature is quite
adept at making me look stupid and it took a while
for me to realise that the noise was in fact being
created by a small army of frogs – literally hundreds
of them scuttling around in a pleasingly captivating
manner. On spotting me they would dart under the
water, perhaps cautious that I was a supplier for a
French Bistro.*

Head on up the rigg, and as the path forks, take
the left prong behind a wooden swing gate. As this
grassy track heads slowly downhill, fabulous views
of Glaisdale open up ahead. There is a through road
in the dale, but it is so steep as it descends from the
heavens, you'd end up in Denmark if your brakes
failed. Accordingly, the valley is quiet and serene and
great for walking.

With skylarks chattering and lapwings swooping,

Signs of industry in Glaisdale.

carry on more steeply downwards past a disused quarry. Go left over an ancient stone bridge – presumably for the old rail or road access to the quarry – then very quickly right and continue to descend next to a wall. Two yapping dogs in the adjacent farm will confirm that you are on the right track.

One-hundred of your imperial yards before reaching the road, go left through an iron gate into the churchyard of Glaisdale Methodist Church. 19th Century headstones – perhaps in memory of somebody who worked in those old quarries – indicate that living into your 80s is not the modern concept that we think it is.

Daffodils near the Methodist Church.

Head right along the road – illuminated in springtime by Wordsworthian hosts of daffodils – and after a minute or so a signposted path runs down through some trees and over a stile before going diagonally to Plum Tree Farm. Immediately behind that stile I was confronted with spring once again as I almost trod on a ewe that had just – and I mean just – given birth to twin lambs. It looked me up and down and gave me a stern look as if to say: "I'm kinda busy, pal. So do one." (I humbly deferred and went the long way round to the farm).

Lambing at Plum Tree farm.

Walk through the centre of the farmyard, then onwards across the dale to a footbridge over Glaisdale Beck. One-hundred of your metric metres after the bridge, go through the left of two gates, panic at the sight of 200 newly hatched bumble bees, then go uphill through two more gates to Low Gill Beck Farm.

An old farmer (I really should have jotted down his name), spent a pleasant 15 minutes with me explaining the personality traits of a rare breed of sheep and telling me about the dale, it's history and people and the best places to spot wildlife. That may

not initially sound captivating, but let me tell you that I was enthralled. Perhaps that was because, just the day before, I had to battle to stay awake during a conversation with a friend 30 years younger than me. He was extolling the virtues of his new phone – particularly the App he'd downloaded telling him how far he was from his nearest Big Mac and Fries, (though to be fair, he would probably starve to death without it). He's the sort of bloke who would stand at a bus stop and send a text message to Arriva to find out when his bus is due, having found the number to key in at, er, the bottom of the timetable on the bus stop. I think the chat with the farmer taught me a lesson about the difference between knowledge and information.

Turn left along the road, then quickly right at a footpath sign. The path curves left in the field past three old gateposts, then through a gate in a ramshackle wall. Go slightly downhill now to a stone stile, then immediately left through a wooden gate and sharp right along the wall to cross two more stiles. Stay on the same level through two unmarked gates, then straight on towards Bank House Farm.

I was startled to see three heads poking out of the

Looking across Glaisdale.

45

skylight here and it reminded me of an Orwellesque farm in upper Teesdale where I was scrutinized for some time by a sheep – from an upstairs bedroom window. Nothing so bizarre here though – one of these heads was owner Emma Padmore who was showing two friends around her new Bunkhouse conversion. She was kind enough to give me a tour and Emma crucially confirmed that she was hoping to make arrangements to transport guests to and from the pub in the evening.

The path continues straight on through a waymarked gate and soon enters woodland. Emerge through a gate, cross a clearing to a second gate, then over to a wooden shed. Turn left on the track behind the shed, and instead of following it left to head back up the dale, go slightly right and downhill to a marked gate. From here, keep heading down hill and you'll see a footbridge over the beck, leading to a track that snakes right and left as it climbs slowly for half-a-mile or so.

After a left turn through a gate, head towards the buildings on the Daleside, but where a stile ahead leads back to the road, look to your right and you'll see another stile 100 yards away. Cross that and at the far side of that field use a ladder stile and gate on either side of the access road to Hart Hall on your right. Fifty yards into the next field, go right through a gate, then through a stand of seven or eight trees ahead of you, and finally go downhill to the next ridge where you'll see an opening back onto the road that drops down to Glaisdale Station – and that "open all day, every day sign".

Quite recently, this village had three pubs (indeed Northern Trains information board on the station still thinks it has), and the Arncliffe Arms is the only survivor. Curiously, it's the furthest of the three away from the main village at the top of the hill,

46

so it's a long wobble back for the locals. A lot of the trade though, comes from walkers as this pub is on the route of Wainwright's famous Coast to Coast walk. As such it is a popular stopover for through walkers as they gear themselves up for the last leg to Robin Hood's Bay, and you could make lots of new friends by handing out blister pads and knee oil in the bar.

Another great Eskdale pub and once again just a few yards from the train station to get you home.

Arncliffe Arms, Glaisdale.

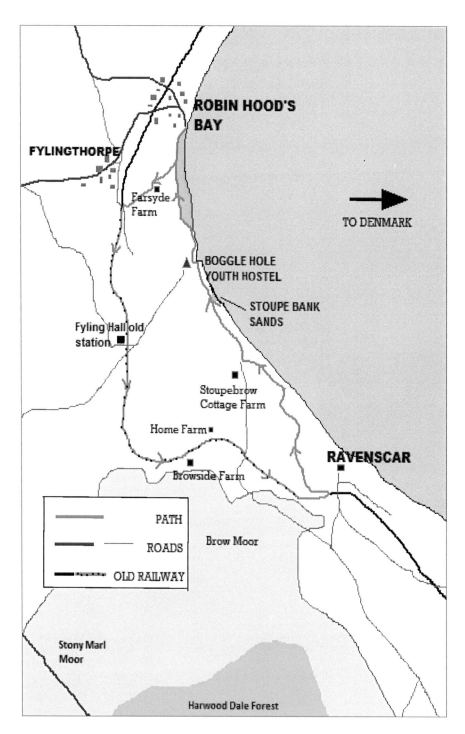

Robin Hood's Bay

DISTANCE: 8 MILES
APPROX. TIME: 3 HOURS
STARTING POINT: ROBIN HOOD'S BAY (TOP OF THE BANK)

It's particularly nice to get away from life's aggravations with a walk through Yorkshire's green and pleasant, and this is a relatively easy eight-mile circular walk between Robin Hood's Bay and Ravenscar. Outbound we'll climb slowly along the old Whitby – Scarborough railway line, and the return route offers wonderful views across the bay as we descend via the Cleveland Way. Along the way there are opportunities to explore local history such as the alum industry or Ravenscar's doomed plans to become a major tourist resort.

I've grumped elsewhere about the hopeless state of the railway industry and how it has deteriorated in the last 30 years (and as I write, Network Rail Directors have graciously declined their 2012 bonus, having to scrape along instead on their six-figure salaries whilst sitting filling in expenses forms in their plush new office in Milton Keynes).

Network Rail HQ, Milton Keynes.

So meanwhile, how are the buses doing? Well I think that the timetabled service is OK considering that most people have their own cars these days, but boy can they get it wrong in real time when they put their minds to it. Arriva took three-and-a-half hours to get me from Redcar to Robin Hood's Bay (15 minutes longer than it took me to get to Corfu in June), and the last leg was spent role-playing a sardine in the 93 from Whitby. It took that long I thought my all-day ticket would expire before I got there.

So, having alighted joyfully from the bus, either go straight down the steep road to the sea admiring the old cottages, shops and cafes, or if you prefer panoramic views take the path on the seaward side of the road which heads down past picnic areas to the sea wall. Head up steps and turn left down a narrow lane to the sea front at the Bay Hotel, where Wainwright's Coast to Coast walkers can often be seen looking tired but slightly smug after completing a 190-mile hike from Cumbria. Go down the alley adjacent to Dollies sweet shop and turn left up steps after the chippy before curling right and upwards to reach the footpath atop the boulder clay cliffs.

Robin Hood's bay from the South.

Soon, where the Cleveland Way heads south through a gate, carry on inland to the pretty pebbled yard of Farsyde Farm and Stud.

Go straight on down the metalled lane to a road junction. Turn right, then quickly left through a wooden gate to access the trackbed of the Whitby-Scarborough railway line. Follow this to your left and stay on the track for three miles all the way to Ravenscar, with lots of fellow walkers and cyclists for company.

You climb some 500 feet along this secluded cinder track in a long avenue of maturing trees, passing Fyling Hall old station on the way.

Fyling Hall old station.

The only diversion required is just beyond the old station platform where a missing bridge means that you have to drop down to cross a road before heading back up to rejoin the old trackbed. Just when you may be growing tired at the lack of a view afforded by the railway cutting, you suddenly emerge near Browside Farm and are rewarded with a fabulous outlook back across the fields to Robin Hood's Bay.

Shortly before reaching Ravenscar, the track

Robin Hood's Bay from Browside Farm.

diverts left onto a distinct paved path. The old railway actually disappears into a tunnel (hidden away in the gorse to your right) hewn from the rockbed by a gang of navvies over 120 years ago, and – goodness knows how they did it – without the assistance of a small army of I.T. specialists, some colourful spreadsheets and assorted men in suits enjoying a nice buffet.

A Scarborough-bound train heading into Ravenscar Tunnel.

By all means head on up to Ravenscar to explore the unfinished village, or perform a Cameronesque U-turn and head downhill on the signposted Cleveland Way path.

Have you ever heard of Geocaching? No, neither had I until alerted by a friend to this new-age treasure hunt game. Essentially, someone hides a "cache" in a dry stone wall, or in a hole in a tree or wherever, then uploads the exact co-ordinates to the geocaching website www.geocaching.com

Enthusiasts then try to find the cache – typically a plastic box of some sort – using a hand-held GPS device and a good old fashioned OS map. Usually, you'd park some way off and enjoy a walk to your destination, then scratch around in the bushes looking for a Tupperware box containing a logbook to sign and maybe some trinket/toy which should be replaced with your own offering.

In the summer of 2011 someone planted such a cache under a seat in Wetherby Town Centre, but they were rather unfortunately spotted by a nervous local who thought "Taliban" and called the Police. They, in turn, called the Catterick bomb squad who cordoned off the town centre for several hours before gingerly opening a small box to find a note saying "Congratulations! Hope you enjoy the fruit gums!"

I mention this because there are a number of caches in the Ravenscar area, and I spent some minutes vainly poking around near an old brickworks before realising I was at my furthest point from the pub and hastily giving up. Good fun though, and if it gets people out walking – and maybe a little treasure hunt would help to get the kids involved – all well and good.

120 or so years ago, when Ravenscar was known as Peak, enterprising (if slightly mad) Victorian entrepreneurs attempted to create a resort here to rival Scarborough. They laid roads and sold plots of land for house builders, but crucially turned a blind eye to one terminal problem. The Victorians loved to dip their dainty little toes into the sea and at Scarborough they could do so after a quick shuffle across the foreshore road to the sandy South Beach. At Ravenscar, they'd need to walk 600 feet down a dodgy path that had been cut into cliffs, before arriving at a particularly unimpressive stony beach. Then they'd look around forlornly for a cliff lift and

realise they'd have to walk back up again. Not surprisingly, there was little interest and the plans for the Ravenscar Riviera were ditched.

The street layout is still there to see and a few stretches of the cliff path haven't fallen into the sea if you fancy heading that way. I recommend a parachute and oxygen.

South Cheek and Ravenscar.

OK, back at the walk, having done your u-turn, head downhill and where a sign indicates the route to those old brickworks, you should instead bear right and continue your journey back to the coast. A further diversion goes off to the old alum works whilst the wide main path takes you back to the Bay. One decision you need to make is whether to walk the last mile along the beach (accessible at Stoupe Bank Sands or Boggle Hole), or along the cliffs to that gate you passed at Farsyde Farm just above Robin Hood's Bay.

The tide could make that decision for you, but if you do manage to get along the beach, look out for ammonites and Whitby jet in the Jurassic rocks (there are precious few dinosaur bones unfortunately, though their fossilised footprints have been found in the area). Beware though, if you find something interesting in a *Tupperware* box, someone may have got there before you.

Boggle Hole.

The seashore route soon goes from rock to sand and after leaping across the beck at Boggle Hole, you will soon be sidestepping sandcastles and dodging frisbees as you get closer to the ice cream van next to the Bay Hotel.

Whichever way you go, the cafes and pubs of Robin Hood's Bay await in this idyllic little village next to the sea. Enjoy!

Below and right – Robin Hood's Bay beach.

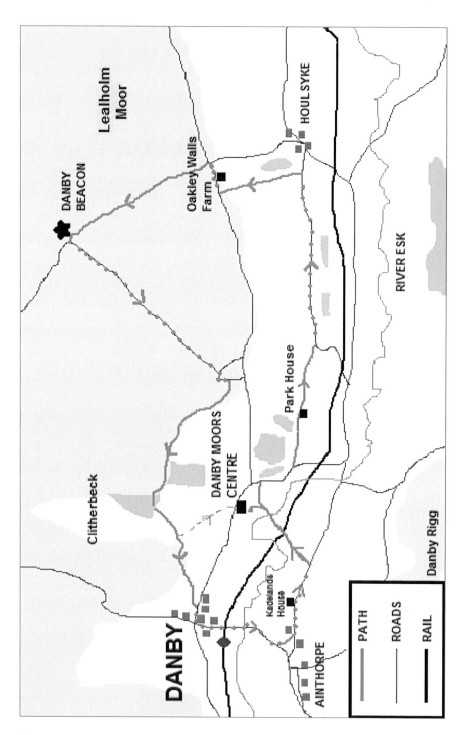

Danby Beacon

DISTANCE: 6.5 MILES
APPROX. TIME: 2.5 HOURS
STARTING POINT: DANBY STATION

The lofty moors around Danby Beacon are often the recipients of North Yorkshire's first winter snows. So, if you're planning to tackle this six and a half-mile circular walk from Danby in autumn, it's time to tunnel through that pile of old shoes and carrier bags in the bottom of your wardrobe, in the hope of locating the weatherproof jacket you threw in there last April.

Six-and-a-half miles is not too far, but there is one serious, calf-stretching, 500-feet climb from the valley floor up to Danby Beacon. Halfway up the hill, you will begin to realise that the manufacturer's assertion that your jacket is "waterproof and breathable" is a triumph of marketing over functionality but, thankfully, the views emerging all around you will be more than adequate compensation for a soggy shirt.

The summer of 2011 was cancelled due to the recession, so it was nice to start from Danby Station

Monkey Puzzle Tree at Danby Station.

on a warm but hazy October day. Turn right on the main road and cross the rail and river bridges.

From the latter I saw what I thought was an otter at the water's edge. Maybe I should have gone to Specsavers, but it seemed too large for anything else as it scuttled up and down the riverbank, before disappearing under the bridge and refusing to come back out. Perhaps it was spooked by the big lummox leaning precariously over the parapet and was nervously looking for roadside signs showing a weight limit for the bridge, or maybe it just swum off in search of lunch. I tried to get over a fence to take a closer look, but succeeded only in lacerating my arms in the bushes and eventually gave up, with the otter/stoat/weasel by now halfway to Whitby.

Info point at the Moors National Park Centre.

Moors National Park Centre, Danby.

One-hundred yards after the bridge, take a signposted path on the left leading uphill to quickly join Easton Lane. Turn left down this minor road and enjoy the views of Danby Rigg and Danby Castle in the distance. Shortly after dipping down to pass Kadelands House, take a signed path left and follow the track over the railway line, then up to a bridge over the river into the grounds of the incongruously named Moors National Park Centre.

This is a visitor centre run by the North York Moors National Park, and here you'll find a series of indoor and outdoor attractions/activities based around moors life, crafts and the environment. Art exhibitions, trails and play areas, a climbing wall, quoits, sculptures, guided walks, and so on, attract visitors from far and wide. There is also a tourist information centre/shop and an excellent cafe where I enjoyed a pot of tea and a rather pleasant fairy bun (© Larry Grayson). The centre and cafe remain open throughout the winter, though opening times are limited after school half-term in October, so you should probably check.

You've only walked a mile-and-a-half, so finish your tea and get cracking by heading right on the main road from the Moors Centre, passing the car park on your left. One-hundred yards or so after bending left, go through a gate in the hedge on your left signposted for Lealholm, then diagonally right uphill to the wall in the far corner. With the wall on your left, cross a couple of stiles and follow the path above Park House to soon enter a farmyard with more dogs than you can shake a stick at. And you probably shouldn't. The track soon joins a metalled road which you should follow for a mile or so rising slowly uphill and revealing lovely views of Eskdale and Little Fryupdale away to your right.

View to Little Fryupdale.

This tiny road leads to the village of Houlsyke which, as a friend of mine reminds me every time we pass it on the train, is the only sizeable hamlet in Eskdale without a pub. I do wonder what happened though to the guy who, a few years ago, reportedly set up a microbrewery in Houlsyke. Perhaps he drank the lot himself and is still snoring on the settee with a slice of pizza stuck to his shirt.

Shortly before the road dips down to Houlsyke, a signed path on your left (slightly to the right of a wider track and partially hidden behind some trees), leads up to a ladder stile over a wall. If it's not

raining, remove that plastic jacket and brace yourself for a long slog uphill keeping a wall to your left and head through two gates before emerging on to moorland where you soon turn right on a minor road to spend quality time gasping for breath. As you admire the view across the valley, pause to consider why the human body, on reaching 50 years of age, begins to judder and creak like the Tin Man in the *Wizard of Oz*.

Various inspections from the NHS equivalent of a Customs baggage scanner, have confirmed that I have significant arthritis around my ankles and knees, together with (and I quote directly from my medical record) chondral eburnation, meniscal extrusion, and semimembranosus gastrocnemius bursa, drizzled with a beetroot jus and served with a parmesan crisp. I showed the diagnosis to the Occupational Health Nurse when I worked on the railway and although she nodded in a serious and knowledgeable manner, her eyes flickered from side to side before she retired to a back room and presumably "Googled" it. She returned with the helpful advice that "it means your knees are worn out and you have to give up anything you enjoy".

Quite why the human body thinks it's a good idea to stick all your joints together as you get older, I don't know. Perhaps I don't drink enough beer.

After passing Oakley Walls Farm on your right and opposite where a gated-road leaps down the hillside to your right, turn left on a wide track into the heather. You will soon see that this leads directly to Danby Beacon, standing proudly at the highest point in the distance.

The Beacon dates back to the 17th Century when it was first erected to warn of a marine invasion from the French, then the location had a lease of life as a radar station in the Second World War when it was instrumental in tracking the first enemy aircraft to be shot down on British soil. The wooden beacon eventually had to be replaced and in 2008 it was carefully rebuilt in steel, to reflect local history and industry. The vantage point affords wonderful views across to Scaling Dam, flotillas of French warships in the North Sea, and also inland towards the high moors of North Yorkshire and North to the last few puffs of smoke from industrial Teesside.

Danby Beacon in winter.

After a gentle mile downhill on the road to Danby, with stunning and panoramic views ahead to Castleton and the Fryups, the road suddenly turns sharp left. Shake off any pursuing Gallic warriors by taking a path to the right alongside the stone wall ahead of you. (There are two signed paths heading

View towards Castleton.

Footbridge over Clither Beck.

right before the one you need to follow, so make sure you are on the track that hugs the drystone wall). Follow the path/wall as it turns left then downhill to the secluded valley of Clitherbeck. Cross the stream at the bottom of the hill using a footbridge 150 yards to the right of the wall, then bear left over a stile and diagonally up to a gate taking you into young woodland.

Emerge into an open but uncultivated field through a second gate, then go right and uphill to pass through another gate in the wall at the top of the field. Head on uphill through bracken to soon meet a wider track which heads downhill to Danby.

This neat and pretty village has a lovely health food shop and, behind it, a slightly less healthy but equally lovely bakery and cafe. Here you can enjoy a good value lunch, gallons of tea and select from a small medley of confectionery, pastries and macho equivalents of the visitor centre's fairy buns. 30 yards further on is the Duke of Wellington Inn which I heartily recommend for the second time in this book. (That should earn me a free pint, surely?)

Duke of Wellington, Danby.

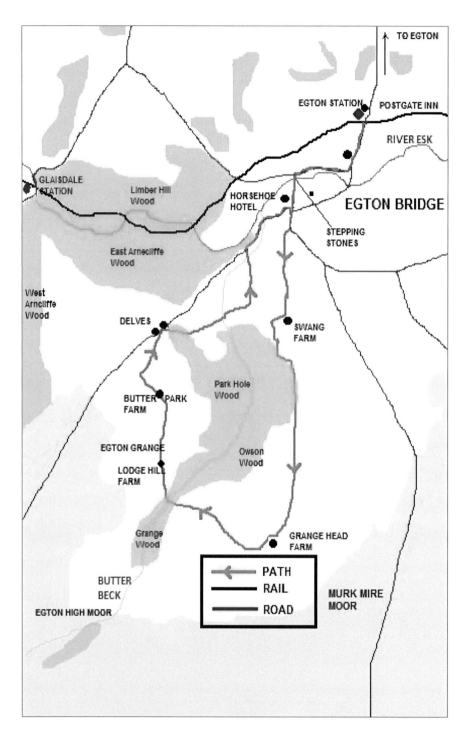

Egton Bridge

DISTANCE: 5.5 MILES
APPROX. TIME: 2 HOURS
STARTING POINT: EGTON BRIDGE STATION

"The Delves, Egton Grange" sounds like a four-bedroom bungalow in a cul-de-sac in Ingleby Barwick. In fact it describes the lovely, shallow, wooded valley hidden away to the South of Egton Bridge. This gentle, two-hour walk begins at Egton Station which is accessible on the brilliant M&D 99 bus from Whitby, or of course, by train.

Leave the hordes of bored brats on the train screaming: "Are we there yet, Mam?" to some disinterested woman staring at her mobile phone, and walk down the station approach towards the main road. Resist terminating your walk after just 20 yards, by turning your back on the excellent Postgate Inn, instead heading right along the road under the railway bridge.

Egton Bridge is a lovely little village, nestling by the river half-a-mile down the hill from its big sister, Egton. Now, whilst travelling around the world, if the top three must-see items on your list are huge trees,

Postgate Inn.

Belgian paintings and gooseberries, then you are in luck. The village holds one of the few annual gooseberry shows in the country in early August, and in 2009 the world record largest gooseberry (a pie-sized 62 grams) was shown here. There must be something in the soil, because on your right, just after the church, there are some colossal trees in the gardens shooting up like proverbial beanstalks into the blue. And the Belgians? Well, if you can, go inside St. Hedda's church and check out the paintings around the altar – not to mention the lovely

Gardens behind St. Hedda's church.

St. Hedda's Church.

roof decorations, which fall somewhere between my living room and Michelangelo.

Take the road right after the church and 300 yards further on, as the road kinks right, look out for the "To the stepping stones" sign on the wall on your left. A short path leads down to the river through the very obvious infrastructure of an old water mill, before heading across the Esk on two sets of stepping stones. (Check the map for an alternative route along the road from St. Hedda's chuch should the river be in flood, or if your knees are made exclusively from jelly).

When I crossed, after two months of drought in

Old Mill on the Esk.

the spring of 2011, I would barely have got my boots wet if I'd fallen in. But despite the lack of water in the river, the trees were alive with birdsong and I watched in admiration at 30 or more swifts gathering mud for their nests at the water's edge – perhaps their only Jewson's for miles around.

After emerging near a road junction, (and mentally clocking the inviting pub down to your right), carry on straight ahead, uphill on the main road signposted to Goathland. After 30 yards, head right on a signed path into the bushes, soon over a stile, then bear left uphill with a ramshackle wall/line of bushes on your left. Ignore a track heading to your right and head steeply uphill adjacent to the bushes and a wire fence.

Cross a stile and head up to a gate, (or use another stile 20 yards to your right), and follow the well-defined track behind it, to your right. Keep right at a fork in the track through a few holly bushes, then past a derelict barn on your left that is just begging for an owl looking for a new pad. Carry on through a waymarked gate into a little avenue of trees, then down a wide track heading south to Swang Farm.

I've only ever walked this path twice and a curious

thing happened to me on both occasions. As I passed that derelict barn, a pack of hounds in Hall Grange Farm way down in the valley, began baying wildly as if about to be released by the resident Kommandant. But, on looking down the slope, I watched a solitary Labrador charge up the path, leaping majestically over stiles, and it eventually appeared 30 yards behind me on the footpath. Both times, it looked me up and down for a few seconds, before turning tail and bounding away back downhill to report to HQ. If you see it, do say hello from me.

Towards Egton Grange.

Just before Swang Farm, go right through a metal gate and head down and slightly left in the field, swerving past a group of confident-looking cows like a 737 avoiding a thunderstorm. A waymarked gate away to the left provides a route through to a wide track with lovely views, that runs for a mile or more before bending right to Grange Head Farm.

At the farm buildings, go through a wooden gate on your right and (keeping a small stream on your left), head downhill through two gates. Next, it's diagonally right across a field to another marked gate then downhill into thin woodland before crossing a footbridge over a stream. Follow a track

69

for a short distance, but then leave it to climb steeply left and up a grassy lane to the farm above, where a marked wooden gate takes you into Lodge Hill Farmyard. Your guess is as good as mine as to whether or not it's inhabited. If it is, the net curtains could do with a wash, to be honest.

Keep on the same track as it snakes on and through Butter Park Farm, then a few hundred yards after the farm buildings go right at a junction in the track. When you reach the road at the Delves, turn right and then almost immediately right again along another signed path which is very popular with the local nettle community.

The path drops steeply down and crosses a track (two stiles), then continues to descend through a field to a footbridge over Butter Beck. The name of the beck, when coupled to my urgent need for a beer AND the fact that this is the only place I've seen an owl in broad daylight, immediately brought Harry Potter to mind. However, if you are one of the few people in the world never to have heard of him, you won't know what I'm gibbering on about. (Nor will you understand why a Ford Anglia is flying down the side of the page).

By the way, If you have seen the Potter films and have a few thousand pounds earning no interest under the mattress (or earning no interest in the bank, because the four per cent you thought you were getting went down to 0.1 per cent as soon as you walked out of the door), I heartily recommend a trip to the Wizarding World of Harry Potter at Universal's Islands of Adventure in Orlando. But be warned – pack the kids off to summer camp or put them in kennels or something. Orlando is no place for youngsters.

Harry Potter Land, Universal Orlando.

Head slightly right and uphill to a gate, then up through bushes to a stile leading to a wide track. Packs of dogs and a curious Labrador are nearby on the right, so head left to eventually join the road leading downhill to Egton Bridge.

After a ford in the road, you soon come to the Horseshoe Hotel, Egton Bridge's second superb pub. Excellent ale, great food and a lovely beer garden in one; great food, excellent ale and a lovely beer garden in the other. I couldn't name one pub in the whole of Teesside as good as these yet the tiny hamlet of Egton Bridge has two! Unfortunately, the winter in 2010 did them no favours financially. I was told that in a very snowy ten-week period, The Horseshoe attracted the grand total of eight customers. So do yourself a favour and use one or other of them before they disappear for good.

You can route back to the station via the stepping stones again, or go back along the road and over the "new" bridge (the old one got washed away in a storm), or for a little more adventure, flag down a passing Ford Anglia.

Horseshoe Hotel.

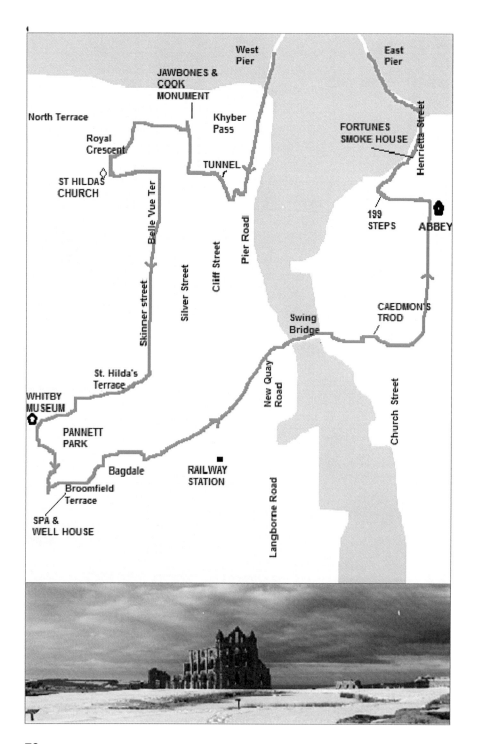

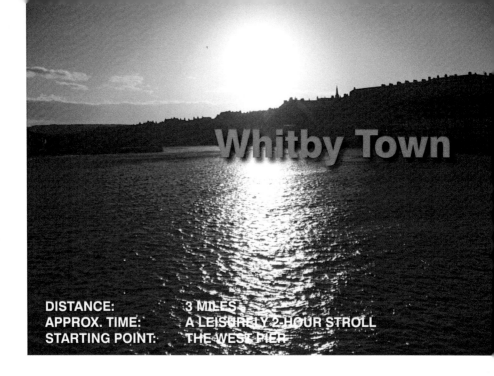

DISTANCE: 3 MILES
APPROX. TIME: A LEISURELY 2 HOUR STROLL
STARTING POINT: THE WEST PIER

This walk around the manifold attractions of Whitby, is in honour of my mam and dad. My mam would book the family holiday when I was a kid, and when her favourite stretch of railway line from Whitby to Scarborough finally shut down, Whitby became the preferred destination. She made all the decisions like that and looked after the money that my dad earned in his 48 years at Smith's Dock shipyard in South Bank. He was just happy to finish his shift, hand over his wage packet, tend his tomatoes, and settle down with a bottle of home brew in front of the black and white telly. He also happened to be the nicest bloke I ever met. Mam died aged 88, a few weeks before I penned the article for the *Whitby Gazette* and I figured it would be nice to dedicate a walk around their favourite holiday spot to their memory.

I write it with affection and not a little envy for those who live there. For me, Whitby is still a lovely

place and hasn't really changed in 50 years. So you can do this three-mile stroll in your trainers, as we are on pavements the whole way. It may be particularly attractive to visitors on a weekend break who wish to spend a couple of hours escaping down some of the back streets and seeing some of the sights that don't involve a deep fat fryer.

Starting from the West Pier, head along the quayside past the Lifeboat museum. Soon you get to the amusement arcades, where the only person you are likely to see emerging with more money than when they went in, will be wearing a Securicor uniform.

In the 1960s, with my mam and dad enjoying themselves up the road in the Buck Inn, my brother and I would spend many an hour feeding our pocket money into one-armed bandits and exciting new "wheel-em-in" machines, which, if you happened upon a flooky success, would grudgingly fire half-a-dozen pennies at you as if from a cannon.

My memory tells me that it was a Whitby arcade that displayed a sign saying (with all the sincerity of

Left to right: Jim and Betty Instone, myself, Jenny and Syd Bell (Mam and Dad). Circa 1962.

74

Between two of the largest arcades a flight of steps leads up to an alleyway. Follow this to the left, then after 20 yards turn right up a path and steps that

take you to one of the most photographed locations in the town. The view back through the Khyber Pass tunnel perfectly frames the Abbey on the opposite cliff and is a lovely place to pause for breath.

Go through the tunnel, across the road, then head right to the iconic whale's jawbones, symbolic of Whitby's whaling history. The current archway was erected in 2002 after the originals had to be removed due to advanced decay that could not be

Khyber Pass Tunnel.

fixed by the massed ranks of the town's dentists. The originals – much bigger than the current arch which is from a smaller species of whale – were taken away and languished in a builder's yard in the Esk Valley,

Whale's jawbones.

before suddenly appearing for sale on e-bay. After something of an outcry, they were kept in the area after being handed to the owners of Raithewaite Hall Hotel (they made a suitable contribution to a charity). By all accounts, they are not in great nick, but hopefully they can be preserved and maybe erected at the hotel's entrance drive on the coast road to Sandsend.

Standing proudly a few yards away, is a statue of Captain James Cook. At school, my imagination only had a forward gear. History was boring and irrelevant. Now though, I find it fascinating to think that James Cook himself would have regularly stood on this spot, contemplating journeys into the unknown. Most of us think it's the height of exhilaration and risk management to spend a couple of quid pootling around Sandsend bay for half-an-hour in a replica ship with an engine. What a man James Cook was, and how exciting must it have been to be aboard the Endeavour in the 18th Century.

Head up the coast and turn left along the impressive Royal Crescent. Turn left again along Crescent Avenue, then soon down Hudson Street. This is guest house country with names like "Rosslyn" (presumably owned by Ross and Lynne) and Abbey House (Abraham and Beyonce).

Turn right at the next junction and go straight on into Skinner Street, with its gift shops and tea rooms. Botham's is Whitby's answer to Betty's of York (or maybe it's the other way around), and the upstairs tea room is quaint and old fashioned in a way that the prices aren't. Actually, it's no more expensive than many of the town's other cafes, so treat yourself to a pot of tea with Yorkshire Brack (a fruit tea-loaf) and demand a ride on the stairlift on the way out.

At the end of the road, turn right onto St. Hilda's

Captain James Cook.

Whitby Museum, Pannett Park.

Terrace. A few hundred yards up the hill, go past the entrance to Little Park and enter Pannett Park through a blue gate. A path up to your right takes you to Whitby Museum. Inside you'll find exhibitions on the geology and natural history of the area, as well as homages to Captain Cook, William Scoresby and others. Scoresby and his imaginatively-named son William Junior, were whaling captains and they brought back numerous artefacts from their trips to Greenland. Now, if whalebone carvings and Inuit kayaks don't push your buttons, ask about the Tempest Prognosticator.

The Tempest Prognosticator.

Invented in 1850 by Doctor George Merryweather, a Whitby doctor, the Tempest Prognosticator was designed in the style of an Indian Temple and consisted of 12 pint bottles set around a circular stand, under a bell with 12 hammers. Each bottle contained a live leech and a piece of whalebone attached to the bell hammers by a wire. The grand plan was that changes in atmospheric pressure and electric charge presaging a storm, would spook the leeches into climbing to the neck of the bottle where they would dislodge the pieces of whalebone and ring the bell at the top of the device. It was meant to be used on ships where a sudden burst of Mike Oldfield's Tubular Bells *was a hint to the skipper that a huge storm was approaching and he may wish to change course or at least retire to his bunk. Oddly enough it didn't really catch on – perhaps Dr Merryweather is a distant relative of Michael Fish.*

The Museum will cost you the price of a pint and a packet of crisps (and last a lot longer) after which you should head down steps opposite the museum entrance and take a path downhill which curls right to the restored lily pond and shelter. Carry on down to Bagdale and turn right before crossing at a safe place near the roundabout, before doubling-back to take a short diversion right after Baileys Accountants.

This is Broomfield Terrace and halfway down on the left is an unusual spa and well house (originally water from the spa was going to be pumped up to the aforementioned lily pond, but the money was never found to make it happen). I understand that the inside of the well house is fabulously ornate and is occasionally opened to the public by the Civic Society, but it's a shame that from the outside it just looks like a shed with a funny roof.

Spa and Well House.

Cross back over Bagdale, up the steps, then quickly right downhill past a number of churches, built with such huge sandstone blocks that it looks like they were expecting an earthquake. Turn right then quickly left down Whitby's main shopping street, emerging at and crossing the swing bridge over the river.

Swing Bridge.

Turn right along Grape Lane in front of the *Whitby Gazette* Office (pausing to slip a note in their letterbox complimenting the "Stroll with Stuart" column), then left at the end after the jet shops, cafes and Captain Cook Museum. Resist the temptation to head left to go in Hadleys Fish Restaurant (my

Grape lane.

favourite), and instead cross the road then go left for 20 yards before climbing the steps on your right called Caedmon's Trod.

At the top, turn left on a path between the Abbey buildings and the area known as the Donkey Field (previously a grazing area for beach donkeys but also apparently a haven for frogs and rare newts) before heading into the grounds of St. Mary's church. This ancient church is worth a visit at any time, but especially so in

December when it is decorated with hundreds of Christmas Trees. Head down the 199 steps and at step No.1, turn right along Henrietta Street past the fabulous Fortune's kipper house. Kids – if you get the chance to look inside the smokehouse make a mental note that this is what your lungs will eventually look like if you keep on smoking behind the bike sheds.

Fortune's kipper house.

Journey's end is 200 yards further on, where you descend on to the East Pier, just a 100 wet yards away from where you set off.

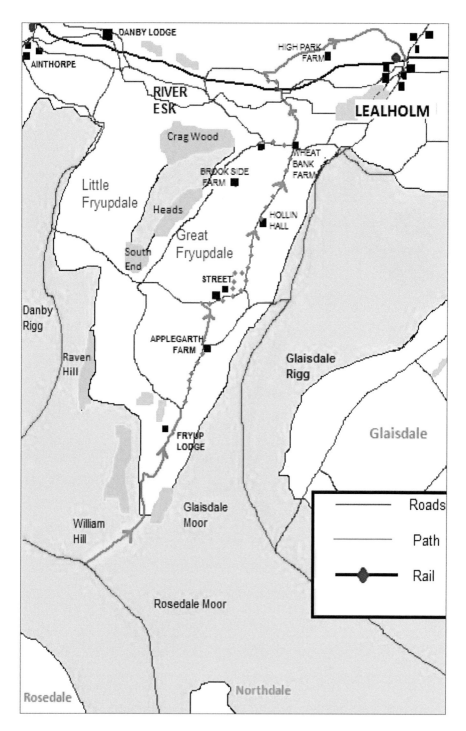

Great Fryupdale

DISTANCE: 9 MILES
APPROX. TIME: 3.5 HOURS
STARTING POINT: MINOR ROAD ON EAST SIDE OF ROSEDALE (ACCESSIBLE BY MOORBUS)

All of my walks are accessible by public transport, largely because I don't own a car, but also because they usually end in a country pub where I can be found making a futile attempt to rehydrate with alcohol and salted nuts. I also try to plan circular walks so that you can choose to use your own transport in case, like my sister, you haven't seen the inside of a bus for 45 years.

Well this time, tough. It's a nine-mile linear walk down the length of Great Fryupdale, which means that you'll get to see the entire valley from the wild and precipitous slopes of the headwall, down to the gentle, rolling contours near the junction with the Esk. You can get to the start point on Sundays by using the superb Moorsbus Network (if it's survived Cameron's axe by the time you read this), and once Northern trains grudgingly admit that winter is over you can catch a Sunday train home from Lealholm. Northern trains "summer" service typically starts two

*Moorsbus at
Ralph's Cross.*

months after you've finished your Easter eggs, and ends three weeks before the last Test match at Lords.

Leave the Moorsbus at a footpath crossroads a mile past the turnoff for Fryup on the road to Rosedale Abbey from Ralph's Cross. Head north on a distinct path through the heather, then curve around William Hill (but don't expect to get a bet on the 2.45 at Chepstow). Occasionally an old stone trod emerges from the peat, but after half-a-mile it vanishes into a boggy area which will have you planting each footstep in a meticulous manner. As the stones reappear you can lift your head to see that a wonderful vista has crept up unnoticed – a spectacular view down the length of Great Fryupdale.

Any deluded fool suggesting that Fryupdale is somehow linked to greasy breakfasts, should be treated with compassion and generosity should you meet him along the way. In common with the Scandinavian derivation of Lealholm, Danby, and the like, Fryupdale owes its name to Viking invaders who, having alighted from the Moorsbus, were so impressed with the view that they named it after Freya – the Norse goddess of beauty, love and destiny.

Drop down onto a wide crosspath – part of Wainwright's famed coast-to-coast route – and turn right. After 50 yards or so, turn left along a thin path behind a large cairn. The path soon drops steeply down to the valley floor, but before tackling it pause and take in arguably the most awesome view in the North York Moors.

*Majestic View down
Great Fryupdale.*

You'd be forgiven if you questioned how the piddling little streams and becks that drain Fryupdale managed to carve out such wide, grand and beautiful scenery, mirrored in its neighbours Danbydale, Westerdale and Glaisdale. Well, many years ago, I got A-Level Geology and Geography at Middlesbrough High School, and after a long career working in such essential and popular commercial functions as Human Resources, I.T. support and Health and Safety Management, I'm glad to get a chance to hazard an educated guess at something interesting.

So, with a little help from Wikipedia, here goes. Some 20,000 years ago, the North York Moors were covered in a huge sheet of ice, hundreds of feet thick. As the earth warmed up (let's blame the Chinese), the meltwater carved out these wide valleys. Some bigger torrents – often released when an ice dam holding back a lake collapsed – created even bigger features, such as a route through the cliffs for the River Esk to escape at Whitby, or the wide and steep-sided Newtondale, home of the

83

North York Moors Railway. It sure would have been a long train journey to Pickering without all that ice.

Left and below: the headwall of Great Fryupdale.

The path heads north, curling left over a stream and up into bracken, before levelling out after a gate as a clear grassy track. Half-a-mile later, pass through an unmarked wooden gate on a lesser-used route to the right of the main path. Bear left through the middle of the field and head left to keep a farm building on your right. A wide track soon becomes a metalled road through Fryup Lodge and on for a mile to Applegarth Farm.

As the road turns sharp right through the farm buildings, go straight on along a wide track. After passing through a second gate (a metal one), go almost immediately through another unmarked metal gate in the wall on your left. You can see a footpath sign in the wall diagonally opposite, where you drop down onto a minor road and head right to the tiny hamlet of Street.

Looking West over the dale.

The dale is spectacularly beautiful, but the paths are hopelessly unmarked as if the recession has resulted in a world shortage of waymarks. Accordingly, I'm going to suggest that you now follow the road through Street and onwards for two miles to Wheat Bank Farm. I followed a field path for a while, but a combination of tied-up gates and unmarked stiles made for slow progress. Several unsavoury outbursts aimed at anonymous farmers/landowners who keep their spare barbed wire on stiles, echoed across the dale. Some of them employ other little tricks too, such as tying up gates with twine on rights of way and using Houdini-proof knots. Or spending thousands of pounds landscaping their property so that years of slurry accumulates next to the footpath sign. In the North York Moors National park though, it's unusual to find such problems, and the Viz-style "Get orf moy laand" red-faced old man with a shotgun, lives elsewhere. Annoying though, on this long walk on a hot day, but I think it's still appropriate for me to apologise for the language.

Anyway, by all means drop down across the dale to route via Brook Side Farm if you wish (good luck with that), or take my tarmac alternative which is just as pretty and virtually traffic free.

Halfway down the dale.

At the road junction in front of Wheat Bank Farm, turn left then quickly right down a track. After half-a-mile or so, fork right then quickly emerge into a field. Drop diagonally right to the lowest part of the field and cross the River Esk on hamstring-tweaking stepping stones. Whoever laid them got his/her calculations slightly skewiff, and as you near the far side, you need to look out for a larger gap between two of the stones. Tip the water from your boots before heading up towards a wooden barn, then it's left to the field corner, over a stile and on to the road.

More steppings stones over the Esk.

Looking back from the rail bridge.

Summer and Winter, Lealholm Station.

Turn left over the railway bridge, then 300 yards later take a stile on your right and head diagonally right, almost doubling back on yourself. Keep straight on through a series of stiles and gates and follow the direction of the waymarks (wahey!!) to the next stile which is always visible in the hedgerow opposite. Well, it is until you overtop High Park Farm where you should just keep the fence on your right and the next stile is hidden in the corner of the field.

With the fence now on your left, drop steeply down to the woods, over a footbridge, sharp left at a stile and curve left and up to a further stile. Head diagonally right in this field which is cruelly uphill at this stage, and with the fence on your right cross a final (honest) stile at a spaghetti junction of footpaths. There are lots of signposts here and with wisps of smoke coming from my left knee, I took the path sharp right which soon curves left directly to Lealholm Station.

Cross the track through kissing gates at the end of the platform, then downhill into this vibrant village showcasing a cafe that epitomises the term "suntrap", a lovely bakery, a popular garden centre and a lively riverside pub – The Board Inn. (Superb food and ale served by busy hosts Karen and Alastair). A band on the pub patio, kids paddling in the river, sun beating down. Fantastic.

Board Inn, Lealholm.

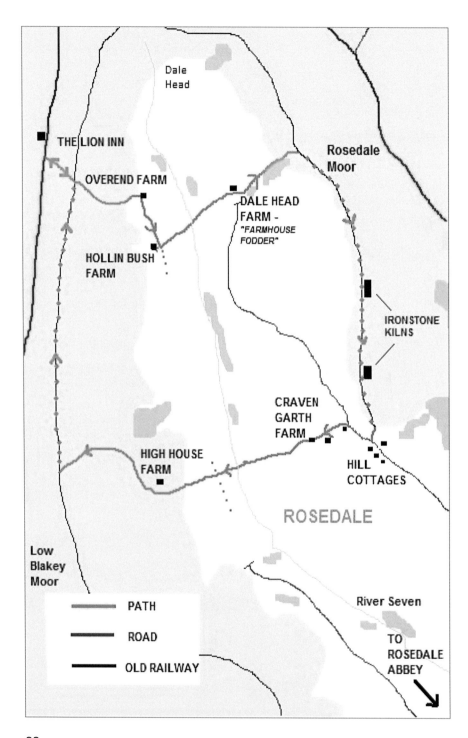

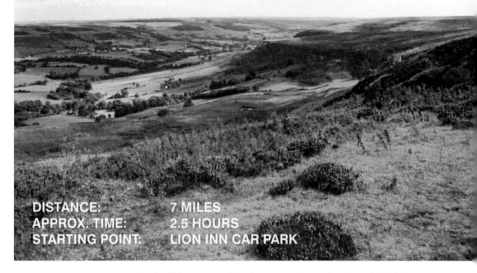

Rosedale

DISTANCE: 7 MILES
APPROX. TIME: 2.5 HOURS
STARTING POINT: LION INN CAR PARK

With nature having a variety of colourful tricks up her sleeve towards the end of summer, I very much recommend an August Bank Holiday walk on this route around upper Rosedale. It's essentially quite flat but does include one Olympic-level climb and features a wonderful cafe in the middle of nowhere, as well as industrial ruins and beautiful moorland and valley scenery. Oh, and take your cozzie because there's a hot tub and sauna halfway round. If you only do one walk in this book, then this is probably the one to do.

I went by Moorsbus (available on Sundays until the end of October), and started the circular walk from the Lion Inn – the iconic and ever popular pub high on Blakey Ridge. The Moorsbus, if you've never heard of it, is a network of bus services sponsored by the North York Moors National Park. (Well, as it's largely public money, it's sponsored by you to be honest). They've been ferrying people from Hull, York and Teesside up to and around the otherwise bus-free dales and moors for many years but, sadly, lots of men in shiny suits and Bentleys have probably scuppered that. In 2014, austerity measures mean that the buses will be replaced by two donkeys and a tuk-tuk.

With the pub behind you, take the path 20 yards to the right of the cottage opposite, leading diagonally down to the valley. After 300 yards or so cross straight over the old ironstone railway on a thin path just visible to the right of a small gully, heading downhill as if on a bee-line towards the farm in the distance.

The path soon becomes more obvious as you continue to descend through heather into a cleft on the valley side. After half-a-mile or so of deep purples and olive greens, vivid splashes of scarlet lit up the valley as I passed two berry-laden rowan trees, and whilst the colours will vary at different times of the year, I guess they will always be similarly stimulating.

You soon emerge on to a wider track snaking

Upper Rosedale.

down to the valley in a series of hairpins (cut the corners off if your ancestors were mountain goats). Go through the gate into Overend Farm and turn right along the track. Half-a-mile later at Hollin Bush Farm (Hollin is a Yorkshire dialect word for Holly), leave the wide path that heads right and go straight on through a gate to turn sharp left downhill in a field.

Footbridge over the River Seven.

Stay to the right of the dip in the centre of the field, then cross a footbridge over the tiny River Seven, up through the next field, through two gates and then left on the minor road. Now, prepare yourself for a treat and a half.

You are at the head of a remote valley with no through road, with bracken and heather climbing skywards on three sides. Now be honest, is this where you'd expect to find a fabulous cafe serving superb home-made fare and Yorkshire tea in bone china? Maggie Barraclough opened "Farmhouse Fodder" at Dale Head Farm a few years ago, and now has parties of walkers planning their day around a visit to this hidden gem. The views are wonderful, swifts flit around between the parasols in the garden, and it's just an outstanding place to eject your rucksack and watch nature getting on with her daily

Farmhouse Fodder.

chores. There's even a quaint little shelter just in case the heavens choose to open on your teacake.

Opening times are limited outside of the summer months, so check ahead and even on a cold November day you may be able to sample Maggie's home-made soup in that little shelter. If the winter of 2011 is repeated, you may be lucky enough to get snowed in until February.

Drag yourself away and head through the gate marked "Fryup" (it's not the truckers' entrance) opposite the cafe garden. This path climbs steeply up beside a wooded gill, to reach the old ironstone railway which has taken the easy route round from the Lion Inn. Turn right and head south for two miles. With several sheep looking down on you like Apache scouts, pass the old roasting kilns, where the ironstone was baked to concentrate the iron content.

This industry was at its height in the second half of the 19th Century and, without a Thai businessman in sight, supplied the fledgling iron and steel industry on Teesside. Redcar's steelworks has recently been reopened by Thai firm SSI, who realised that they may be able to control costs rather better than the previous owners, who had fallen into a well-used, not to say text-book, trap of allowing decades of consistent trade to take their eye off the

Sentries.

Ironstone Kilns.

ball. Suddenly, the combination of a world recession and cheap supplies from new steelworks in India and South East Asia, exposed their cost control techniques as something akin to an eight-year-old boy in a sweetshop.

The old rail track terminates at a curious stone shed, around which someone appears to have made several attempts to recreate the final scene in *The Wicker Man* – either that or they're planning an extravagant party on bonfire night. Go through the gate to the left of the building and down the stony track, past a duckpond to the Daleside road.

Turn right and after 100 yards you come to The Orange Tree Relaxation centre, where you can have a Sauna and Jacuzzi should it tickle your fancy. (That last bit isn't actually on the menu). What a wonderful and diverse place Rosedale is – and if you fancy staying a few nights, there are some super places for rent after you quickly turn left down a track marked Craven Garth Cottages.

Rosedale Abbey is a few miles down the road, where a selection of cafes and pubs await your debit card. It's an attractive and low-key touristy little village befitting its position at the foot of this spectacular dale.

I first went there as a teenager when two friends

and I got hopelessly lost attempting the Lyke Wake Walk – the famous 42-mile trek from Osmotherley to Ravenscar. We went the wrong way at the Lion Inn and ended up staggering across the moors in the dark in the general direction of Pickering. If I ever need a reminder that I have an extra stupidity gene, I just have to think of that night. We set off in steady rain at 3.00pm, wearing trainers and denim jackets, and none of us had a map. By 2.00am, with the rain still slanting down, hypothermia was setting in and we only survived by descending into Rosedale Abbey and finding refuge in a shed at the back of a pub. At seven the next morning, we emerged into warm sunlight and sat on a fence to dry out. When the landlady opened the door to bring in the milk, she was greeted by the sight of three clouds of steam in her garden, one of which drifted over to ask if there was any chance of a pot of tea. Looking like a frightened extra in Doctor Who, *she barred us out of her pub for life and slammed the door.*

Later though, we enjoyed a wonderful breakfast (two breakfasts each actually), then spent several blissful hours in another pub not giving the remotest stuff that we should have been 20 miles away in Ravenscar.

Head straight on through a gate in the farmyard and continue downhill through a second gate to eventually recross the River Seven on a footbridge. Climb uphill to reach a wide crosspath which, if you turn right, will ultimately take you back to Overend Farm, below the Lion Inn. For better views, head straight on through a gate, up through a gap in the next fence, then curl round to a ladder stile in the top right corner of the next field. From here, supplementary oxygen needs to be considered as you follow a fairly distinct path heading steeply upwards through the bracken.

A flatter, boggier stretch marks the boundary

Across Rosedale to the kilns.

between bracken and more lush heather. The path heads up and then right, before curling away left (ignore the OS map which shows the path heading off to your right) and relentlessly into the stratosphere to once again turn right onto the railway track.

From here, it's a gentle 30 minutes back to a little wooden fingerpost that you passed three hours ago marked with the words: "Lion Inn", where – smelling delightfully of lavender and talc (but only if you had the Jacuzzi) – lunch awaits.

Moorscopter at The Lion Inn, Blakey Ridge.

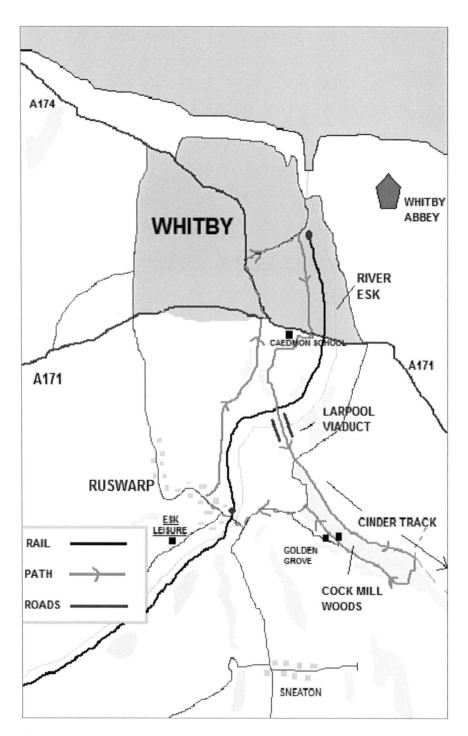

WHITBY

A174

WHITBY
ABBEY

RIVER
ESK

A171

A171

CAEDMON SCHOOL

LARPOOL
VIADUCT

RUSWARP

CINDER TRACK

ESK
LEISURE

GOLDEN
GROVE

COCK MILL
WOODS

RAIL
PATH
ROADS

SNEATON

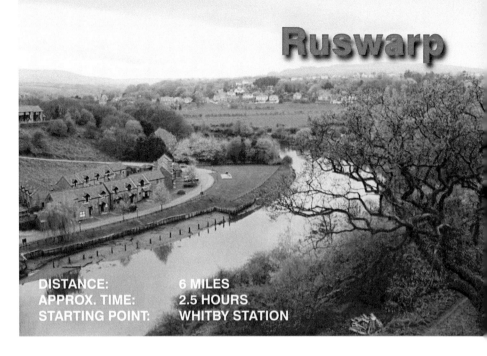

Ruswarp

DISTANCE:	**6 MILES**
APPROX. TIME:	**2.5 HOURS**
STARTING POINT:	**WHITBY STATION**

This circular walk between Whitby and Ruswarp, takes in an architectural triumph, vintage British woodland, a hidden waterfall and an indoor play area near the end as a carrot to entice the kids out for a walk. I'll also indulge myself with a short excursion down memory lane.

Starting at Whitby Train Station, turn sharp left up Windsor Terrace, passing those two staples of British life, a curry house and an off-licence. Stay on the lower level of this road as it passes some new cottages on the left, with names such as "Sleepers" and "Clickety-clack" indicating the proximity of the Esk Valley railway line. It's a pleasant residential area of the town rarely visited by tourists.

As the road curves away right, head up the steep asphalt footpath ahead. The path diverts down steps on your left in order to pass under the A171 Scarborough Road.

Before doing so, I passed a guy managing to

walk more slowly than me, possibly because of the 12-pack of Stella *he was lugging up from the Co-op. As is customary, I said: "Morning," and he responded with an indeterminate primeval grunt, a snarl of derision and a general demeanour that it was somehow my fault that his head was made entirely of bone. Thankfully he was not typical of the sort of people you may meet and greet on my walks.*

Presumably he was headed for the underpass below the bridge where the mountain of empty lager cans suggested to me that aluminium is available in commercial quantities for some enterprising mining conglomerate.

Soon however, you climb back up to civilisation as the path runs parallel to the road before turning left at Caedmon school. With the school on your right and a house on your left, head through a gap in the fence onto the school playing fields, then turn sharp right with the fence on your right.

After 400 yards, just after the school long-jump pit (go on, have a go – you know you want to), drop down and head left on the cinder track – the redundant (I know the feeling) Whitby-to-Scarborough railway line. This beautiful route was one of many that made Dr. Beeching's eyes light up as he sat staring at a rail map of Great Britain armed with the 1960s equivalent of a bottle of Tippex. At a stroke it was gone, probably saving enough money to pay a week's expenses for the planning committee of the M25.

Invited – and handsomely paid – by the Conservative government of the day to use a set of shears on the British Rail network, Beeching destroyed nearly 4,000 miles (honest – 4,000 miles!) of lines like this all over the country, many of which were subsequently reopened by volunteers with restored steam locomotives. (Kind of a forerunner of

Dr. Beeching.

Cameron's "Big Society"). For political balance though, I should add that just a few years ago Alistair Darling, Labour's Transport Secretary before he was asked to shuffle decimal points around as Chancellor of the Exchequer, also explored the idea of lopping more miles from the network. "We are not in the business of transporting fresh air around the country," he said, with the aid of a smug grin. Now, the pendulum has swung back again with the proposal to build a new high-speed route through the heart of England, (recommended by a Network Rail "investigative report" which I guess they'd have sneakily loved to call "Kerrching"!). It should make a lovely cycle path sometime next century.

Larpool viaduct.

You soon reach the majestic Larpool viaduct. Its 13 arches and five-million bricks stand 125-feet above the River Esk and the low parapets afford stunning views on either side. The last train ran over the structure in March 1965 (you'd think they'd have tried to make a few bob from the summer season) and was fenced off for years before the whole route was opened as a very popular cycle/walk-way virtually all the way to Scarborough. It passes treats like Robin Hood's Bay and the remains of the evocatively-named station Hayburn Wyke, which served nothing much more than a nearby hotel and a rocky beach.

Cross the Viaduct and carry on down the old track with the imposing 215-year-old Larpool Hall Hotel gazing down on you away to your left.

Left to right: my brother Steve, Mam Jenny, myself, sister Sandra and friend in a camping coach at Staintondale.

In the 1960s, I used to holiday down here in camping coaches at places such as Cloughton and Staintondale. They were old railway coaches done out with bunk beds and powered by *Calor* gas. With the toilet 100 yards away in the station buildings, I suppose it was a bit primitive even for the 1960s, but still a lot posher than the carriages Northern Trains currently use on the Saltburn-Darlington line.

My brother and I would be left in the evening with a pile of *Superman* comics, some Whitby rock, a packet of *Smith's* crisps and the station goat for company, while my parents disappeared to the Shepherd's Arms for three hours. They'd get arrested nowadays for child neglect, but I have nothing but sepia-tinted memories of family holidays that were always too short and made me cry on the journey home.

Left to right: Steve, Dad and me at Hayburn Wyke.

The Cinder Track.

After a mile or so of gentle walking with woodland on either side and decorated in springtime with bluebells, lesser celandines and, some pretty white things that weren't daisies (I know, I should get a book), you come to a small stone bridge with steps on your left leading down to a footpath fingerpost. If it's not a small stone bridge and it doesn't have a footpath sign, you aren't there yet. If you are still on the track when you reach the village of Stainsacre, you've gone too far.

The path through Cock Mill Wood.

Double back under the railway line and head downhill through the gorgeous Cock Mill Wood. Cross a footbridge over Stainsacre Beck (almost dry on my visit after seven weeks without rain), then up the other side bearing right until you come to a wide track and a gate labelled: "Watson's Farm". Head right down the track which soon turns into a metalled road, and after a mile or so you'll reach the impressive Cock Mill Hall (stop sniggering at the back) in the tiny hamlet of Golden Grove. The road heads left over a bridge, but you should go straight on past what look like renovated stables and left down a stone track into the woods.

Within yards, stop and feast your eyes on Waterfall Cottage, and its wooden decking overlooking the falls on Rigg Mill Beck. Subdue your jealousy and make a mental note to buy another lottery ticket before heading on down the path. Keep the beck always on your left and after ten minutes or so you'll emerge on the minor back road from Whitby to Ruswarp. Turn left to reach the latter in just under a mile, but be careful as the road has no pavement for pedestrians.

Boating on the Esk at Ruswarp.

Cross the river bridge at Ruswarp then head left down the road towards Sleights where, after a few hundred yards, you can hire rowing boats and canoes on a long and calm stretch of the river. If you're with your family and know you won't be able to resist attempting a qualifying time for the next Olympics, but subconsciously feel the need to protect your kids, there is an indoor adventure playground and a nice outdoor cafe just across the road – the rest of the family can go there while you frighten the ducks. There's also crazy golf, an animal petting farm, pottery painting and something called Laser Tag (no idea – I'm 57). If all that's not enough, further down the road is a good old-fashioned miniature railway, whilst in the other direction is the Bridge Inn.

When I popped in the Bridge for a sneaky one, the menu included something called the "all-day belly-buster breakfast". This consisted of an entire farmyard fried in lard, a toasted white loaf, a pot of tea and the phone number of the emergency doctor. A quick look at the tungsten thread holding the Landlord's waist buttons in place showed that he had personally tested this epicurean feast several times, but I do caution that you'd have to walk on to South Africa to get rid of the calories.

OK, done with Ruswarp? Back on the main road, head up the hill towards Whitby, but quickly escape from the increasing gradient by turning right along a path just past the Butcher's shop. Stick to the paved path as it bears left across a field and uphill into woodland. Keep on uphill through a metal gate and just keep following the stone flags ignoring some other clear tracks to either side. After a few minutes you will emerge on the A171 which you can follow downhill back into Whitby to buy that extra lottery ticket.

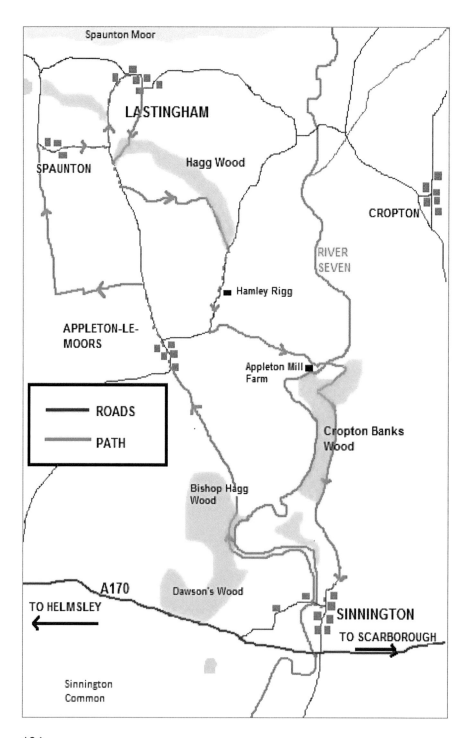

Lastingham and Sinnington

DISTANCE: 9 MILES
APPROX. TIME: 3.5 HOURS
STARTING POINT: SINNINGTON

A left knee that fails to perform its primary function of bending in the middle, had kept me indoors for a while. I therefore had to thank the succession of pompous and superior oafs on daytime TV for sending me hobbling out of the front door to enjoy this lovely walk on the gentle southern slopes of the North York Moors. As an extra bonus, I treated myself to an optional excursion to Pickering.

The BBC seems to have made several million episodes of a show where some pillocks scam a free holiday to Australia, pretending that they may move there. Then, with the assistance of an onion, they blub uncontrollably at a video of their friends back home even though they've only been away for three days, and decide instead to stay in their six-bedroomed bungalow in High Wycombe. By switching aggressively over to Sky, you can watch cultured alternatives such as a woman making some cakes, or a man in overalls renovating an old motorbike in his back garden. Then there's the cookery show I saw where some snobby food critic, confronted with a dish of duck breast on a bed of puy lentils and spinach, described it with a snort of derision, as "the sort of thing you might knock up for supper if you don't have much time". Yeah, right. Not from my fridge you won't.

Meanwhile, ITV has Jeremy Kyle.

Aaaaaaaaaaaaaagh!! Let me out!!!

2 good reasons to go out for a walk.

Start at the cute village of Sinnington, (served by the 128 bus from Scarborough to Helmsley and also by the Moorsbus Network), head for the hills and cross the bridge over the River Seven. Immediately turn right and follow a track alongside the river. After half-a-mile or so the path heads left and starts climbing until you go through a gate on your right marked: "Path to Appleton". Follow the woodland trail with the river initially babbling away some distance below, then emerge through a gate into a field and follow the path as it curves left to a gate in the bushes ahead.

Back to Ryedale from Appleton-Le-Moors.

The route is now straight uphill through two gates into the village of Appleton-Le-Moors, but pause on the ascent to look back – through clouds of Red Admiral butterflies on my visit – across the fields to Ryedale.

Walk straight on through the main street and half-a-mile after the road turnoff for Cropton, take a

Red Admiral and friend.

signposted path through a field to your left. Cross a stile 20 yards to your right in the next hedge boundary and continue heading west for five minutes until, after a small jigsaw of hedgerows, you turn right on a wide track eventually leading to the sleepy hamlet of Spaunton.

Go right for half-a-mile, and on reaching the road junction, turn left downhill to the gorgeous village of Lastingham. If you have time, take a look at the 11th Century St. Mary's church. The architecture, the windows and especially the crypt are fascinating whether or not you embrace religion. And whoever you worship, I'm sure a donation wouldn't go amiss.

St. Mary's Church, Lastingham.

Just opposite the church, is the superb Blacksmith's Arms. Another donation here would see you rewarded with excellent real ale and food in one of the small rooms or in the lovely beer garden.

The walk back to Sinnington is prettier than the walk up, but if your lunch was too liquid, you could – like me – get so hopelessly lost that you will have to abandon ship halfway through and come back the following week. Eight miles in seven days is an average speed of 80 yards an hour, more or less the pace of an arthritic tortoise. Don't worry – I know where I went wrong. Follow the road through Lastingham (pub on your left), and after it snakes right and then left again, head up a side-road to your right.

Lastingham.

Curve left and uphill towards farm buildings and take a path signposted into woods on your right. Follow this up and left to come out on the road. Head left down the road for 200 yards, then through a gate on your left passing Oldfield pond. Head diagonally right towards two trees, then through a metal gate to follow a field track keeping the fence on your left.

Turn right then left around the perimeter of the next field, then right along the top of an escarpment at Hagg Woods admiring the view across the valley to Cropton Banks.

Gradually descend through woods on carpets of beech nuts and pine needles – with a small feathered rug denoting a fox's breakfast bowl – and turn right along Howldale Lane. Follow this minor road to the

Looking East over Hagg wood.

right for almost a mile until, after it climbs right and up through trees, it heads off sharp right towards Appleton-Le-Moors. Instead, turn sharp left down a metalled road with views over to Hamley, all the way to Appleton Mill Farm.

Looking North, above Appleton Mill Farm.

I turned right here, as the map seemed to indicate a river crossing further downstream, but when I reached the river it had transformed into the Mississippi and without an amphibious tank at my disposal I had to retrace my steps back to the farm. We should all learn from our mistakes, but as you will read in another paragraph or two, I managed to pathetically repeat this blunder further downriver.

So, let's assume you've just come down the hill to the farm. Go straight on through a gate and follow a path over a footbridge (the river at this point is a mere puddle by comparison). At the trees ahead, take the signposted path right to Sinnington, through a gate into the woods. This path climbs up through the woods and reaches a crossroads of trails. Head left and up to a path to turn right along Willey Flat Lane. From here, it's a mile or so back to Sinnington along a clear track, bearing left whenever you meet an alternative path.

For the record, I turned right at that crossroads in the woods, and literally and metaphorically went downhill from there. There is an alternative route this way back to Sinnington, but I managed to miss it and ended up on a two-mile cul-de-sac to reach a river crossing which was so deep I couldn't even see the bottom. I tried to hitch a lift on the back of a passing horse but its rider declined my request. Where's Rolf Harris when you need him?

Back at Sinnington, the Fox and Hounds pub won't disappoint, but if you happen to be doing this walk in October and it's the North York Moors Railway wartime weekend, hop on the bus for the short ride to Pickering. This is something I cannot recommend highly enough. There is a bit of a theme in this book where I appear to be making a bid for grumpy-old-man-of-the-year, but I now intend to wax joyfully about this event which attracts thousands of people each year and really doesn't get the publicity it deserves.

At every station along the railway, Dad's Army effectively comes to life. Hundreds – maybe thousands – of people dress in de-mob suits and army uniforms. There are land girls, home guard units and flashy Americans in jeeps smoking cigars with their arms around our women. There are mock conflicts, escaped German prisoners, an 'Allo 'Allo-style Cafe Rene restaurant, music from the era (I

George Formby and Dance Troupe.

watched a quite brilliant rendition of Formby's "Our Sergeant Major" in central Pickering), parades, mock air-raids, jive music and dancing, shops selling wartime goods and much much more. And it's not remotely naff or over nostalgic. What really makes it are the people who dress up as Captain Mainwaring, or some German Kommandant, because they take on the part and stay in character all day performing little impromptu comedy sketches when they meet – "Don't tell him, Pike!"

It really is a brilliant spectacle and a great day out, and it's not just for those of a certain age – the vast majority of people here will have been born long after the war ended and kids particularly seem to enjoy the whole show. A lovely walk in the country followed by a huge and happy show with better entertainment than Sky TV could drum up if they had 5,000 channels. Just marvellous!

Nazis and Allies mingle in Pickering.

111

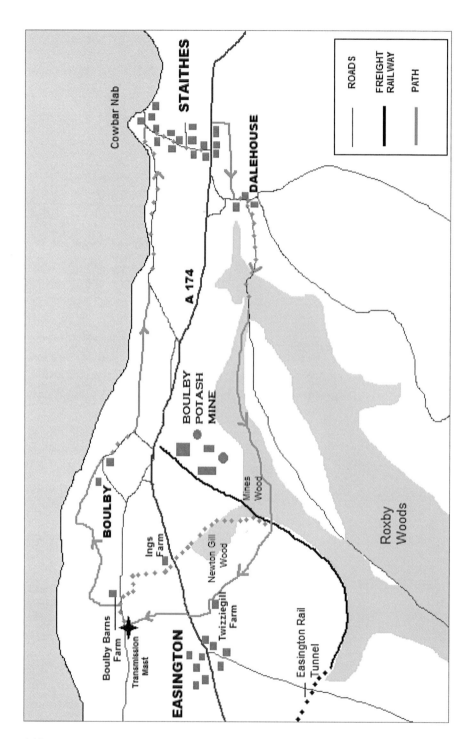

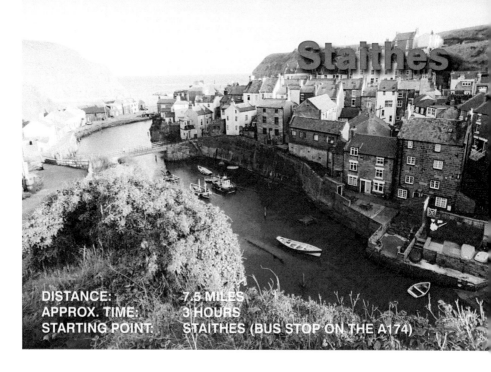

DISTANCE: 7.5 MILES
APPROX. TIME: 3 HOURS
STARTING POINT: STAITHES (BUS STOP ON THE A174)

When alighting from Arriva's X5 bus on the A174 at the top of Staithes village (and you've really got to admire their engineers for keeping these old tubs going), you'd be forgiven for feeling underwhelmed. Pretty it isn't. This end of the village is a modern extension to the old fishing community which is huddled – almost a mile away – around a pretty harbour, and rising up along the side of Staithes Beck. The good news is that you'll see the picture-postcard side of Staithes at the end of the walk.

To start this circular hike, head east along the main road, and on the opposite side to the Co-op, go through a swing gate onto a path by the last of the houses. Just 200 or so yards further on, cross a stile on your right into a wide field. Ignore the half-a-dozen cows that may seem a smidge miffed that you're walking on their dinner, and go through a metal gate at the end of the field, then downhill on a clear track with a fence on your left.

Emerge over a stile into the lovely and hidden village of Dalehouse, and head left down the road. Cross the river bridge, then immediately turn right along Ridge Lane, and follow this narrow road for half-a-mile to go over a ford, then bear left up a hill. Immediately after a "Try your brakes" sign (mine were fine), turn right on a track and follow it for a mile as it heads through woodland, curving slowly to the left.

The track heads right on a man-made embankment over the stream, but before it does so, look left to see a long brick tunnel in the hillside, betraying the mining heritage of this area.

Cross the embankment and turn left to head up to a clearing. Head straight on past a jumble of metal fences and concrete rubble, then climb uphill towards woodland still on a clear track.

The track heads sharp left past a sign saying: "Private woodland – keep out", so do as you're told and head sharp right on a waymarked grass path heading into the woods. Soon you'll find yourself going steeply uphill, and if sliding around in the mud whilst looking desperately around for an escalator were an Olympic event, this is where they'd practice. Mercifully, it doesn't last long and soon you'll find yourself crossing a stile over the railway line that serves the Potash mine.

The path over the Potash Line.

Cleveland Potash have operated this mine since 1969. It is almost a mile deep – so deep in fact that the rock temperature is over 100F. There are a staggering 800 miles of tunnels down there and the workforce needs to be driven for miles underground to get to the rockface deep under the North Sea. Its setting means that it is an ideal place for a laboratory to search for "Dark Matter", an elusive material thought by scientists to make up the hidden mass of the Universe and hypothesized to exist because their calculations don't quite add up without it. Now, I'm no Stephen Hawking, so although I'd like to assist with their search, I probably wouldn't be much use. Recently however, I did enjoy a pint of Dark Matter from the Abbeydale Brewery in Sheffield. I suspect that isn't much help to be honest ... in fact, I'll get my coat.

Now, at this point I'm going to leave you to your own devices. The sensible thing to do is to follow the marked path straight uphill, then onwards to Twizziegill Farm. Follow its access road to cross the A174, then a few yards to the right take a footpath that leads up through four fields to a phone mast half-a-mile or so away. Turn right along a minor road, and wait for me there at a path on your left just in front of Boulby Barns Farm.

Unfortunately, I turned right after the railway line, along a path heading down to Newton Gill Wood. Crossing into the woods, I was confronted with a footbridge that had collapsed more dramatically than the Greek economy. Now this beck is not the Amazon, but I was still there for half-an-hour trying to find a dry crossing.

Dead Bridge.

Steve McQueen in the *Great Escape*, would have said: "It's a fair cop Heinrich, I'm goosed," and given himself up, and wouldn't even have seen the subsequent pile of mud blocking the path, courtesy of several JCBs. I eventually reached the main road looking like I'd crawled out of the sewers. Whichever route you choose, you are afforded lovely emerging views back over the fields to Staithes.

Take a marked track close to Boulby Barns Farm, heading towards the cliff top. After 50 yards you need to cross an unmarked stile into a wide field and head on uphill. Turn right after a final stile onto the cliff top path and essentially keep walking for three miles all

Above: Huntcliff.

Right: Staithes in the distance.

the way to Staithes. The views are wonderful as you drop down (steeply at first) to the lower cliffs and through the few houses that amount to Boulby Village.

Soon you are on tarmac heading towards Cowbar and there are plentiful signs here of the power of the North Sea as the old road disappears into thin air where the cliffs have collapsed beneath it. Your final approach to Staithes is a delight as it snakes steeply down to the small sheltered harbour past handsome cottages and colourful fishing cobles.

Cross the footbridge to explore the old village with it's collection of pubs, cafes and galleries.

Staithes' harbour.

Not much traffic – not even a mobile phone signal – gets down here, so you need to head up the steep hill to return to the bus stop. On the way you'll pass the James Cook Heritage Centre. Cook arrived in Staithes aged 16 to work in a grocer's shop – it's recreated in the Heritage Centre – and it was here that he really developed his love of the sea before moving on to Whitby on the X5.

At the top of the hill, if you have a little time to spare, is the Captain Cook Inn where the fire blazes, the banter is good, the beer is superb and the furniture, carpet and other sundry decorations are still awaiting delivery. A unique place – perhaps best summed up by recalling that the Landlord recently held his own mock funeral procession and wake because he didn't want to miss the booze up. Just don't expect cocktails and cucumber sandwiches.

Poster in the Captain Cook Inn.

On the way in to this unusual but very friendly pub, you may have to say "excuse me" to the usual gaggle of punters who have popped outside for a smoke. It's a scene repeated at every pub doorway in the country since the smoking ban was introduced. I welcomed the ban with open arms and not just because there was finally some reason to justify voting for Tony Blair. Far too many times I've had to have a bath and change all my clothes after returning from a pub reeking of Benny Hedges, and for years I whinged impotently to my boss about having to sit in a blue haze all day in the office. Surely, in 100 years' time, they'll be aghast that decades after discovering that smoking tobacco will likely kill you – even telling you explicitly on the packet – you could still buy them in the corner shop. They may as well sell plutonium in the Post Office.

So, I've been waiting for a chance to tell the nation how to solve this problem once and for all. Here it is – and remember, when it becomes official government policy, you read it here first. **Fanfare of trumpets please, maestro...**

■ *Raise the legal age limit for smoking by one year.*
■ *Do the same every year.*

SIMPLE! It means that if it is legal for someone to smoke now, it always will be. And if it is illegal for someone to smoke now it always will be.

It also means that tax revenues will only slowly diminish and tobacco companies will have time to slowly diversify to other products, or do what they're doing now and concentrate on killing the Chinese. When you've finished mulling over this faultless plan whilst sipping your Martini in the Captain Cook, head up the road past the excellent chippy, to catch the bus back home.

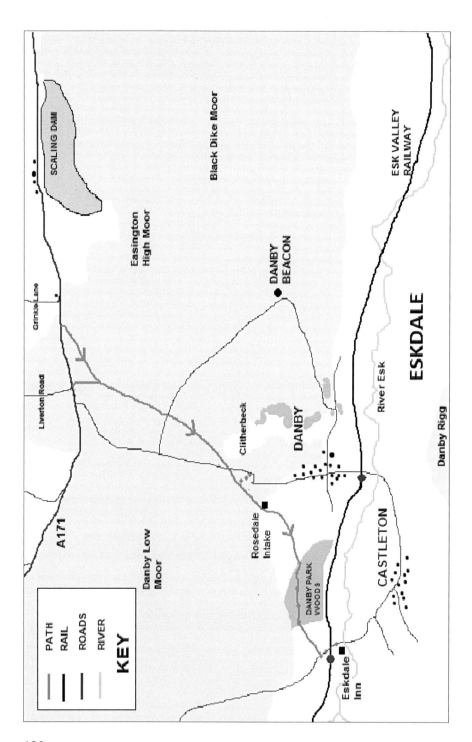

Across the moors to Castleton

DISTANCE: 5 MILES
APPROX. TIME: 2 HOURS
STARTING POINT: LIVERTON ROAD END – ON A171

In the last chapter, I asked you to do a bit of navigation for yourselves, chiefly because I got lost halfway through. You may have to do the same again on this one, because I've done it twice now and gone wrong both times! I include it though because this was my first column for the *Whitby Gazette*, appearing in late 2010. I had lots of time on my hands having been made redundant from Redcar Steelworks when they went bust earlier that year.

I was surprised when Jon Stokoe (acting Editor at the time, but now fully-blown Kaiser) invited me down to the office in Whitby, suggested that I write a monthly column and explained that I wouldn't be lavishly rewarded for my efforts. To clarify, you need to think "Big Society" to get a true idea of what he meant – there's not much money in regional newspapers and even less coming back out.

Still, it excited my increasingly moribund brain and I immediately jumped on the 93 bus to reach the start point of this walk, high on the moors a mile west of Scaling Dam. An inauspicious start meant that I got lost within 20 yards, but it all worked out OK in the end …

I recommend you do this walk in late summer, when nature's paint palette majors on purple and mauve. I'm sure though that it's gorgeous at any time, as the first two miles see you walking through desolate moorland carpeted with heather, before dropping down to rural Esk Valley and finally through a pretty wood of Silver Birch to reach the village of Castleton. Arriva's 93 bus gets you to the start point at Liverton road end and Northern Trains will get you back home from Castleton station.

Ordnance Survey maps are the best in the world, but sometimes a combination of rampant vegetation and my dodgy internal compass can lead me into parts of the countryside previously only explored by adventurous sheep. I actually started this walk at the end of Grinkle Lane, approximately half-a-mile east of my recommendation to you, and passed confidently through a gate onto the moor. I was soon consumed by shoulder-high bracken which produced some post-watershed language as I stumbled in vaguely

The great Wainwright.

the right direction. Not exactly a great start to my career as an apprentice Wainwright.

With uncannily poor timing, my mobile phone rang and I embarked on a long discussion with a lawyer I'd contacted six months earlier, when I was a smidge miffed at being made redundant from the steelworks. She was hoping to scrape a few bob from a tribunal case for unfair dismissal, but I explained that the moment had now passed and more or less forgotten. I added that the time limit to stake such a claim had in any case expired, that perhaps she should know these trifling details, and that I was slowly sinking into some particularly noxious crimson gloop high on Easington Moor, but thanks for getting back to me so promptly.

I was in the wrong job at the steelworks, but I'm now more grateful that they kept me in beer money for 2 years, than angry at being made redundant. There are some great people there and I wish them well under their new Thai owners.

I rang off to realise that I'd lost sight of the path completely, but after 20 minutes or so, I emerged on to open land close to a prominent boundary stone. To avoid all of these problems, start on the track opposite the Liverton Road, and switch your phone off.

Start of the walk from the A171. Follow the arrow!

123

It's accessed through a little gate below a signpost on the roadside, and after a short boggy stretch just follow the very obvious ditch and dyke running directly away from the road. Now it does soon get a bit tricky because the most obvious path heads straight on, but after 400 yards or so, you need to find another route going off to your right so keep your eyes peeled and stay to the right of the ditch. If you get as far as a raised hummock with the path going over the top of it, you've gone too far so cut across the heather to your right until you find the correct path which is very clear once it leaves the boggier bits, and soon begins to climb slowly to meet, after a mile or so, a solitary Scots pine tree. Er, good luck with all that.

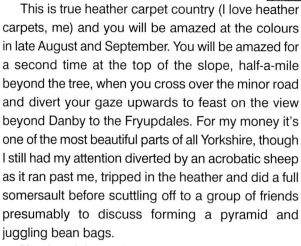

It's solitary existence is quite a surprise on the otherwise featureless moor, but not as surprising as the displays of colourful plastic bags hanging from its branches containing empty pop bottles and *Snickers* wrappers. To be honest, they'd gone on my second visit, so maybe this Scots pine is deciduous

This is true heather carpet country (I love heather carpets, me) and you will be amazed at the colours in late August and September. You will be amazed for a second time at the top of the slope, half-a-mile beyond the tree, when you cross over the minor road and divert your gaze upwards to feast on the view beyond Danby to the Fryupdales. For my money it's one of the most beautiful parts of all Yorkshire, though I still had my attention diverted by an acrobatic sheep as it ran past me, tripped in the heather and did a full somersault before scuttling off to a group of friends presumably to discuss forming a pyramid and juggling bean bags.

Head straight on along the clear track and as you

overtop the valley of Clitherbeck and Clitherbeck Farm, keep a drystone wall on your left before emerging onto the main road down into Danby. After 100 yards or so on the road, take the signposted path back onto the moor on your right. However, there are a number of paths – marked and unmarked – in this area, and if you've gone too far along the road you'll reach a distinct dogleg. At this point you can get back to the correct route by going right on a path just before the road also takes a sharp right.

Either way, you will soon drop down to a farm At Rosedale Intake, where you should follow the blue

Mobile chicken coop.

posts to the rear of the farm building and two benign dogs (well they were until they spotted me).

Bear right past a bizarre mobile chicken coop and head through a pretty wooded section (noting the precarious tree house), before crossing a stream on some convenient large stones.

Climb up from the stream and go left through a gate (despite a confusing waymark suggesting you go straight on), before passing through a second gate and heading left and uphill into the bracken.

Just beyond the farm at Rosedale Intake.

The path remains clear – ignore a wide track heading left – as it heads on alongside drystone walls, but splits in two as once more, it reaches bracken and scrubland. The path straight on will take you down into Danby, so fork right and soon you drop down to a lateral route which, on your right, heads into Danby Park.

The gate into Danby Park woods.

This is a well-established silver birch wood often harbouring a variety of mushrooms that you'd be unlikely to find in your local supermarket. However, unless you are with Ray Mears, I suggest you leave them be. The path continues for a mile or so and after going through a gate and passing a large farm building on your left, drop steeply down to the road adjacent to Castleton Railway Station.

The main village of Castleton is at the top of the hill on the opposite side of the valley and there is a nice cafe, a pub and even a co-op. Mercifully though, if you've had enough, the warm and friendly Eskdale inn is just 20 yards beyond the railway bridge.

This superb and unpretentious pub used to be run by a guy with a distinctly individual sense of humour. A friend of mine, taking his wife to the pub

The superb Eskdale Inn, Castleton.

for the first time, was greeted by the Landlord with: "Now then. Who's this woman? She's nicer than the one you were with last week". Gavin and his wife Linda went off – I think – to Filey, but soon the pub was taken over by two sisters, Karen and Elaine, who brought a new lease of life to the place. Having got rid of several skiploads of Gavin's accumulated junk, the pub is now better than it ever was and worth several hours of your valuable time.

Two hours' walking in gorgeous countryside, lovely beer garden, great food at good prices and excellent real ale with the train station just 200 yards away. What a great place to end this collection of walks. I hope you've enjoyed the scenery and the refreshment stops, have been blessed with half decent weather, and above all I hope I've raised a smile as I've been rambling on, and on ...